Dedicated to Bishop Sherwood Carthen who said at a crucial moment when action, not talk, was needed in order to bring healing to our Sacramento community.

"We're going to build the bridge as we walk on it!"

The Rock of Roseville
725 Vernon St., Roseville, CA
95678 U.S.A.

www.rockofroseville.com

ISBN:978-0-9907171-2-6

BUILDING BRIDGES OF UNITY AND LOVE IN
AMERICA'S MOST RACIALLY DIVERSE CITY

A CITY THAT LOOKS LIKE HEAVEN

FRANCIS ANFUSO

DEDICATION

This book is dedicated to a dear friend who is missed more every day, the late Bishop Sherwood Carthen. He was a principal catalyst for bringing healing to hearts throughout the Sacramento, California region.

One story demonstrates the measure of his influence. During an emotionally charged town hall meeting, called to bring calm to a city in turmoil, numerous city officials attempted to still the angry crowd. None succeeded. In desperation, Bishop Carthen was asked to address the audience.

What happened next showed both the character and influence of the man.

Whereas the house had all but shouted down those who attempted to speak, when the Bishop walked forward, the room quieted. It was a demonstration of trust. He had lived a completely believable life, and, like Jesus, was able to calm the storm.

On another occasion, of which I will write about in detail in Chapter 6, I experienced the wisdom of this gentle giant first-hand. We were away on a retreat with a few pastors when our inability to understand one another threatened to divide us. One revelatory sentence from Bishop Carthen not only cleared the air, but put us on a path we are still walking down even today.

Sherwood, though you are irreplaceable and greatly missed, God continues to unite many from all races and denominations throughout our region. The vision of your heart continues to inspire us.

Till we meet again dear friend,

Your fellow brothers and sisters in the Sacramento region.

For a glimpse into the heart of this extraordinary man, here is a two-minute video link: https://vimeo.com/rockofroseville/review/72308804/49fa034acb

ACKNOWLEDGEMENTS

Two of the sweetest words you and I can ever hear are, "Thank You!" I try to sincerely say them many times throughout my day. But there are moments when two words are not enough. I often feel that as well. "Thank you" doesn't quite cut it when someone runs an extra marathon or willingly lays down their life. At those moments I fight a bad feeling that I have asked too much, especially from those selfless vessels who often give their all. Such extraordinary people surround me! I cannot now think or say, "Thank You" to these giants without emotion flooding my heart. "A Million Thanks" is not even enough!

So in rounding up the usual subjects to thank for this book project, I am especially appreciative that many who have helped me over the years are still willing to climb one more mountain. I give them latitude to say, "No!" but they either have fading memories of how difficult it was last time, or they once again go into "servant-gear" or willingly give their best.

First and foremost, I thank my wife of 39 years. No one says their first "I do" realizing how many "I do's" it's going to cost them. But Suzie's "I do" has been an eternal kiss of support, affirmation, patience and kindness. She is the queen of my life. Not just a pretty face, but a perfect complement for my crazy personality and life. I love you, sweetheart!

My next "Thank You's" will be briefer but no less appreciative: I thank God for the life message and dream of Dr. Martin Luther King Jr., the inspired lives of Bishop Sherwood Carthen and Dr. Joy Johnson, the thoughtful editing of Kathy Kunde, the endless proofing of Lydia Birks, the grace in graphics of Hans Bennewitz, the exacting reference verification of Betty Price, and lastly the comments and corrections of many who read and critiqued the manuscript in one of its life forms.

Without these precious souls stepping up and finishing their stewardships, there would be no book. I am persuaded that one of the benefits of being selfless and unknown on Earth is being closer to God's Throne in Heaven.

FOREWORD

St. Augustine said that HOPE has two beautiful daughters. Their names are ANGER and COURAGE; anger at the way things are, and courage to see that they do not remain the way they are. A City That Looks Like Heaven demonstrates great courage birthed out of great hope.

Francis Anfuso tells the story of Sacramento with personal passion and apostolic authority. Francis has been compelled to author this work by a number of deeply abiding and personal friendships across racial, denominational and gender boundaries – past and present. His writing expresses great joy and humility in co-laboring and sharing a different lens with other men and women committed to the work of building racial unity in the Body of Christ.

Through the prophetic mantle resting on Francis, the world has been given humanizing details, which connect God's call for people of faith to dig the old wells of our forefathers and set the finishing touches of that work in motion today.

This is more than a book to be read—it's a book to be explored. I am honored to have shared in the edits and reviews of the various iterations of this work. As an African American female, who resides in the most diversely populated city in America, I believe this book will set a legacy for many in Sacramento and beyond to reignite a charge for reconciliation that has grown dormant in our culture.

I highly recommend and endorse this book to all who seek to journey beyond the comfortable places and to engage in courageous conversations about healing the hurts and bridging the gaps of our divided society.

Dr. Joy Johnson
Executive Director, Life Matters
President, Sacramento Area Congregations Together (ACT)

ENDORSEMENT

For various reasons and almost by default, pastors often find themselves working in isolation from other local pastors in a city. This pattern is being broken in Sacramento, a city that shines as a true mosaic of ethnicity, color, and culture. It has been our joy to work with other leaders who likewise believe for a citywide transformation. During the last several years, through intentionally drawing together over the simplicity of breaking bread and prayer, we are finding our vital places within our common call to the city we love.

In a culture that grows more consumed with individual followings and public recognition, we have seen true significance arise from thoughtfully preferring and celebrating one another's uniqueness. In this atmosphere of unity and true affinity, we humbly and soberly walk in great expectation for what God will unleash through the fabric of our precious and diverse community.

For this reason we affirm the focus and intent of this important book. God's hand is on Sacramento in such a marvelous way, and we believe this volume will be a catalyst for its further transformation.

Pastors Don and Christa Proctor — *City Pastors Fellowship*

Rick Cole — *Senior Pastor, Capital Christian Center*

Greg Fairrington — *Senior Pastor, Destiny Christian Church*

Samuel Gordon — *Chair, MLK Celebration Committee*

Scott Hagan — *Lead Pastor, Real Life Church*

Lance Hahn — *Lead Pastor, Bridgeway Christian Church*

John Jackson — *President, William Jessup University*

Joy Johnson — *Executive Director, Life Matters Inc.*

Jeff Kreiser — *Director, The ACTS Group*

Parnell M. Lovelace, Jr. — *Founding Pastor, Center of Praise Ministries*

Samuel and Eva Rodriguez — *Senior Pastors, New Season Christian Worship Center*

Sam Starks — *Executive Director, MLK365*

Alex Vaiz — *Senior Pastor, Vida Family Church*

INTRODUCTION

A moment of great clarity is called an epiphany. The word, derived from the Greek word for revelation, finds its origin in the manifestation of Jesus Christ as the Savior and Son of God. It commemorates the moment the three wise men (magi) recognized the baby Jesus, God come to Earth.

This book has its origin in an epiphany, a revelatory moment when God touched my life. It was June of 2011, and I had gone away to pray and fast for a few days thoroughly burdened over the condition of the church and culture in America. I was fully persuaded that unless there was a move of God, an outpouring of God's Spirit, a revival, an awakening, America would go the way of much of Europe, not becoming just a post-Christian nation, but more and more anti-Christian.

I had brought with me books on revival and some of the biographies of great Christians, evangelists and revivalists I had read over the years. Though I did not have time to reread them all, I was able to review the sections I had marked and the comments I had made spanning four decades. Kneeling down near the end of this consecrated time, I acknowledged these epiphanies before God:

1. Though revival is a supernatural act of God, there were clear biblical and historical dimensions that I could obediently pursue in preparation for God to revive the Church before awakening the lost.

2. My part required nothing less than a whole-hearted abandon to Jesus.

3. There would be grave dangers before, during, and after the moving of God's Spirit. I needed to prepare to face them.

Now, a few years later, I am still in pursuit of God coming to Earth, and in particular where I live, Sacramento, California. Jesus is moving here in a uniquely magnificent way! The unity and camaraderie of church leaders across racial, denominational, and geographic lines is at times astounding. But is there something we can do to feed the hunger God has placed within us to see an outpouring of His Spirit? I am fully persuaded there is! It begins by fearlessly identifying and focusing on our most serious challenges, which are really opportunities in disguise. God gets no greater joy than doing the impossible. That's why we are thrilled to watch Him move.

He has made Sacramento, America's most racially diverse city, for a grand purpose.[1] It is not a coincidence that many sense we are on the verge of something extraordinary. New levels of relational connection and bridge building are occurring throughout the region. We are so grateful to God!

Heroic invitations await each of us. Though this book will not provide a step-by-step blueprint on how to bring about a move of God, it intends to fan the flames of love, faith and hope needed to believe for the miracles that precede revival. It was when the disciples met in the upper room in unprecedented humility and harmony that God's Spirit fell.[2] Sure they were disappointed by their recent failures but they were also filled with forgiveness and overjoyed with God's empowering grace.

The disciples found out what each of us need to know: every irritation is an invitation to go to the next level!

As you read this book, I pray you will be irritated.

I pray that simultaneously as you are provoked to change, you will be emboldened to re-dig the wells of revelation hidden within our city and region.

May God touch Earth where you live, and may you never be the same.

1   Stodghill R, Bower A. Welcome to America's Most Diverse City. TIME. August 25, 2002. Retrieved from: http://content.time.com/time/nation/article/0,8599,340694,00.html#ixzz2rcHHuep9 on August 9, 2014
2   Acts 2:1

WHY THE BOOK TITLE?

"Use me, God. Show me how to take who I am,
who I want to be, and what I can do, and use
it for a purpose greater than myself."

—Dr. Martin Luther King Jr.

"A City That Looks Like Heaven?"

That's quite a title!

Where is this city? I want to see it!

The patriarch, Abraham, "was confidently looking forward to a city with eternal foundations, a city designed and built by God."[3]

...a nation that looks like Heaven?
Where is that? I want to live in it!

...a person who acts like Jesus?
Where is he? I want to be near him!

Jesus prayed the following prayer to His Father and said we should do the same, *"May your Kingdom come soon. May your will be done on earth, as it is in heaven."*[4]

It was a prayer that will certainly be answered. God's will has always been for Heaven to come to Earth.

So what does God's Kingdom coming to Earth from Heaven look like? The Book of Revelation provides a clear picture:

---

3 Hebrews 11:10, NLT
4 Matthew 6:9, NLT

"After this I saw a vast crowd, too great to count, from every nation and tribe and people and language, standing in front of the throne and before the Lamb."[5]

In the interim we eagerly wait, occupying as He asked us to.[6]

At one point, I wasn't a follower of Jesus, but it was always God's will for me. You could say I was "in process."

If I was driving from San Francisco to New York, and while en route someone asked me where I was going, I wouldn't say Ohio or New Jersey. Yes, I would have to go through those states in order to get to my final destination, but if I forget where I am going I will always wind up in a place I never intended.

WE CAN FOCUS ON WHAT WE'RE NOT, OR WE CAN PURSUE WHO AND WHAT WE ARE CALLED TO BE.

What do you want to see on Earth?

I want to see Heaven!

I want my city and nation to resemble Heaven because firstly this is God's desire.

What do you want to be on Earth?

I want to be like Jesus!

I want my person and character to represent Jesus so well that when people see me they feel like they are looking into the face of Jesus.

Once again, *if I forget who I am created to be, I will always wind up becoming someone less than God intended.* I end this initial section with another quote from Dr. Martin Luther King Jr. It mirrors my hope for the seemingly impossible goal set before us. He wrote it while in jail as a commitment to bring a deathblow to racism and to see his African-American brothers and sisters truly liberated.

---

5 Revelation 7:9, NLT
6 Luke 19:13

"Perhaps I have once again been too optimistic. Is organized religion too inextricably bound to the status quo to save our nation and the world? Perhaps I must turn my faith to the inner spiritual church, the church within the church, as the true ekklesia and the hope of the world. But again I am thankful to God that some noble souls from the ranks of organized religion have broken loose from the paralyzing chains of conformity and joined us as active partners in the struggle for freedom."[7]

THE FATHER'S GREATEST DESIRE

"...like the prodigal son, moved up with some dusty road, his heart palpitating with the desire for forgiveness. But only the injured neighbor, the loving father back home, can really pour out the warm waters of forgiveness."[8]

—*Dr. Martin Luther King Jr.*

What if we really believed God the Father's great desire is for His children to love one another?

What if ending racism in America is not a pipe dream but is God's dream for us?

What if the challenge to love our Sacramento neighbor is really our greatest gift?

Though we have made progress over the decades, we still have a long way to go. Jesus shared what must be our goal, *"...that they all may be one, as You, Father, are in Me, and I in You; that they also may be one in Us, that the world may believe that You sent Me...I in them, and You in Me; that they may be made perfect in one, and that the world may know that You have sent Me"*[9]

I BELIEVE THE VERY SAME THING ABOUT SACRAMENTO'S RACIAL DIVERSITY. IT IS A GREAT TREASURE WAITING TO BE DISCOVERED.

The oneness of Heaven coming to Earth!

That's the goal!

---

7   Letter from a Birmingham Jail, Dr. Martin Luther King Jr.

8   King, Jr ML. Loving Your Enemies. A Gift of Love: Sermons from Strength to Love and Other Preachings.

9   John 17:21, 23

Is it not God's intent to bring the harmony of Heaven to Earth? And might He fashion a template of unity in Sacramento so profound that other cities will be helped as well?

In 2002, Time Magazine ran an article entitled, Welcome to America's Most Diverse City. "In Sacramento everyone's a minority—including whites. Of the city's inhabitants, 41% are non-Hispanic white, 15.5% are black, 22% are Hispanic and 17.5% are Asian/Pacific Islander. Although many cities are diverse (think New York City or Los Angeles), in Sacramento people seem to live side by side more successfully."[10]

As of 2010, Sacramento's ethnic diversity has continued to blossom—34.5% are non-Hispanic white, 14.6% are black, 26.9% are Hispanic and 19.7% are Asian/Pacific Islander.[11]

Has Heaven come to Earth?

Not quite, but it's a good start.

Think of the money being saved by not having to import all of these ethnicities in order to resemble Heaven.

They're already here!

I say this with humor, but also to make a serious point.

The undiscovered gold found in 1848 just a short distance from Sacramento had been there all along and, once found, became one of Sacramento's most valuable resources.

I believe the very same thing about Sacramento's racial diversity. It is a great treasure waiting to be discovered.

We are each in some way responsible to carry the privilege and stewardship of living in such a diverse city. Jesus said as much, *"When someone has been entrusted with much, even more will be required."*[12]

---

10 Stodghill R, Bower A. Welcome to America's Most Diverse City. TIME. August 25, 2002. Retrieved from: http://content.time.com/time/nation/article/0,8599,340694,00.html#ixzz2rcHHuep9 on August 9, 2014.

11 United States Census Bureau. Quick Facts. 2014. Retrieved from: http://quickfacts.census.gov/qfd/states/06/0664000.html on August 9, 2014.

12 Luke 12:48, NLT

MILLENNIALS AND RACISM

"Find some great cause and some great purpose, some loyalty to which you can give yourself and become so absorbed in that something that you give your life to it. Men and women have done this throughout all of the generations." [13]

—*Dr. Martin Luther King Jr.*

In 2014, MTV assessed the social views of thousands of millennials (young people aged 14 to 24) through interviews, focus groups, online panels and surveys.[14] Their findings show a significant shift in the perceptions of those coming of age.

MILLENNIALS ARE "POST-RACIAL."
Seventy-two percent have a stronger belief in equality than older people.

MILLENNIALS BELIEVE IN "EQUALITY."
Eighty-nine percent believe everyone should be treated the same, regardless of their race.

MILLENNIALS COME FROM "NON-RACIST FAMILIES."
Eighty-four percent say their families taught them to treat everyone the same, no matter their race.

(Yet only thirty-seven percent of respondents [thirty percent of whites and forty-six percent of minorities] say they were raised in families that talk about race.)

MILLENNIALS HAVE A "HARD TIME TALKING ABOUT RACE AND DISCRIMINATION."
Though seventy-three percent believe that we should talk "more openly" about bias, only twenty percent say they're comfortable doing so.

MILLENNIALS ARE "COLOR BLIND."
Seventy percent say they don't see racial minority groups any differently than they see white people.

Seventy-three percent believe that "never considering race would improve society."

---

13 Conquering Self-centeredness. Sermon Delivered at Dexter Avenue Baptist Church in Montgomery, Alabama. August 11, 1957.

14 MTV Strategic Insights and David Binder Research. 2014.

MILLENNIALS EMBRACE "DIVERSITY."
Eighty-one percent believe embracing diversity would improve society.

MILLENNIALS BELIEVE "RACIAL BIAS IS PRIMARILY NEGATIVE."
Sixty percent say that most of the bias in their circles is subtle but see it as very negatively impacting despite its subtlety.

MILLENNIALS DON'T WANT TO "FOCUS ON RACE."
Sixty-eight percent say, "Focusing on race prevents society from becoming colorblind."

MILLENNIALS DON'T BELIEVE IN "AFFIRMATIVE ACTION."
Eighty-eight percent believe racial preferences are unfair as a matter of course, and seventy percent believe they are unfair regardless of "historical inequalities."

MILLENNIALS BELIEVE "AMERICA IS STILL RACIALLY DIVIDED."
Though sixty-seven percent saw President Obama's election as a sign that race does not have to be a barrier to accomplishments, sixty-seven percent still believe that America is deeply divided.

MILLENNIALS SAY, "WHITES AND MINORITIES SEE RACE DIFFERENTLY."
Forty-one percent of white millennials say that the government "pays too much attention to the problems of racial minority groups while 65 percent of minorities say that whites have more opportunities."

Forty-eight percent of white millennials say discrimination against whites is as big a problem as discrimination against racial minorities.

MILLENNIALS BELIEVE "RACISM WILL DIE."
Fifty-eight percent believe that as their generation takes on more leadership roles, racism will become less of an issue.

Though forty-three percent of millennials surveyed felt their race was the *first thing* people notice when they meet them, it seems self-evident there are many *first things* we notice about one another: gender, age, attractiveness, attitude, etc.

From this survey you might surmise one of the following:

1. Millennials are naïve to the race issue.
2. Millennials have a better handle on the race issue.
3. Millennials may actually be the generation that solves the race issue.
4. All of the above

The majority of young people surveyed said they want to join a campaign that starts a conversation around bias, thus one purpose and value of this book.

AMERICA: A RACIALLY TOLERANT NATION?

"Our loyalties must transcend our race, our tribe, our class, and our nation; and this means we must develop a world perspective."
—Dr. Martin Luther King Jr.

Sacramento is not just America's most racially diverse city... the United States is considered one of the world's most racially tolerant countries.[15]

Do we know what we have been given...as a city...as a nation?

Is it merely man-made, or is it God-intended?

Can a plant break through asphalt...or does a plant grow through it after the asphalt cracks?

Do our prayers fuel God's heart for a move of His Spirit...or does God's heart to transform our city and nation fuel our prayers? God does nothing just for effect. Everything He does is with intent.

Would God give us a passion to see Him move in Sacramento; would He create a desperate cry in our hearts for an outpouring of His Spirit and a transformation of the church and culture merely to experience the process...without seeing His initiative fulfilled?

---

15 Fisher M. A fascinating map of the world's most and least racially tolerant countries. The Washington Post. May 15, 2013. Retrieved from: http://www.washingtonpost.com/blogs/worldviews/wp/2013/05/15/a-fascinating-map-of-the-worlds-most-and-least-racially-tolerant-countries/ on August 9, 2014.

Is the fact that Sacramento is America's most racially diverse city *an invitation with divine intention?*

Is the fact that Sacramento's forefathers were advocates for racial justice—that they stood up for the rights of the indigent Chinese as well as refused to allow California's admission as a slave state—intended not just to point out our heritage, but to point us toward our destiny?

Sacramento's first pastors put their lives in peril, risked their reputations, and even saw their churches burned because they were compelled by their Creator to stand in the gap for the disenfranchised. More on this later.

Does God intend Sacramento's *heritage* to become our *destiny* and eventually our *legacy?*

WHAT IF ENDING RACISM IN SACRAMENTO AND IN AMERICA IS NOT A PIPE DREAM, BUT GOD'S DREAM FOR US?

What if we brought together Christ-followers from every ethnic group in Sacramento and invited them to reach beyond their borders and comfort zones to meet the needs of another ethnicity? Perhaps even the one they have struggled with the most.

Jesus modeled this so well when He reached out to *tax collectors, Gentiles, lepers, prostitutes, thieves and sinners.* What if this deliberate crosspollination ignited the grace and power of God in our lives and region?[16]

May we not miss our divine invitation...our day of visitation![17]

---

16 Special thanks to Dr. Joy Johnson who provided some of the insights mentioned above.

17 Luke 10.44, 1 Peter 2.12

THE CLEAREST VOICE IN THE 20TH CENTURY STILL SPEAKS IN THE 21ST CENTURY

"Wherever the early Christians entered a town the power struc-ture got disturbed and immediately sought to convict them for being 'disturbers of the peace' and 'outside agitators.' But they went on with the conviction that they were a 'colony of heaven' and had to obey God rather than man. They were small in number but big in commitment. They were too God-intoxicated to be 'astronomically intimidated.' They brought an end to such ancient evils as infanticide and gladiatorial contest. Things are different now. The contemporary Church is so often a weak, ineffectual voice with an uncertain sound. It is so often the arch supporter of the status quo. Far from being disturbed by the presence of the Church, the power structure of the average community is consoled by the Church's silent and often vocal sanction of things as they are."

—Dr. Martin Luther King Jr.
(Letter from a Birmingham Jail, 1963)

Every virtue stands on the shoulders of courage.

Without courage we could not let the God of love captivate our heart, the Prince of Peace be our rest, and the joy of the Lord be our strength.

Without courage we give up too soon, show up too late, and believe for too little.

Bowing to fear is the least safe thing to do. At times, being brave means being courageous five minutes longer or five seconds sooner than those around us. Though we fight weariness, we must hold fast to the call of God on our lives and the promises we have been given. Courage is best seen in a humble Man walking up a hill carrying a cross.

No leader had a greater impact in my youth than Dr. Martin Luther King Jr. Even as I write this, my heart is filled with emotion. It's as if I cannot express my appreciation for his influence adequately. No words are sufficient to express the courage and wisdom I saw in him.

Candidly, I don't even have a runner up.

Dr. Martin Luther King Jr. led the civil rights movement for 13 years, from 1955 to 1968. During his tenure, more progress was made for African-Americans to achieve racial equality than in the previous 350 years.

Somehow, the pure abandon of his life cut through both the national dysfunction and my own personal malaise. Having been abandoned by my own father, it was the clarity of Dr. King's message, and his obvious willingness to risk all, that pierced my struggling heart. When he was cut down by such obvious evil, my appreciation of him only soared.

A flawed man, like each of us and nearly every Bible hero, Dr. King remains the champion of abandon and conviction. Yet, far and away, the clearest representation for racial reconciliation in my lifetime!

When Dr. King was assassinated, like multiplied millions of Americans of all ethnicities, I was completely crushed.

The voice of sanity had been silenced.

I would spend the next two out of three summers living with African-American young people trying to help them sort out their terrible loss.

AN IMMIGRANT'S HOPE

"What is more tragic than to see a person who has risen to the disciplined heights of tough-mindedness but has at the same time sunk to the passionless depths of hard-heartedness?"

—Dr. Martin Luther King Jr.

My father was a mixture of a man.

But then again, aren't we all?

He went from complete obscurity to having his photo on the front page of the New York Times at the time of his death.

My father, Victor L. Anfuso, was born in a desperately poor village, Gagliano Castelferrato, in eastern Sicily, an island conquered by the Romans, Vandals, Byzantines, Islamics, Normans and Spaniards, to name just a few. Sicilians were a defeated, neglected people who, even today, feel the disdain of other Italians. You could say that Sicilians were the Italian version of Samaritans, half-breeds with a mongrel ancestry. Subjugated so often, their plight reminds me of the book title, *"Been Down So Long It Looks Like Up to Me."*[18]

Out of Sicily's tattered past came the Mafia, a word some believe is derived from Arabic, meaning "rejected," or La Cosa Nostra, which means, "this thing is ours," both providing a hint of the grappling for identity of a disregarded and neglected people. They seem to have fulfilled the pattern: *the abused become the abusers; the bullied become the bullies.*

Some, however, chose to break the pattern and fled the island.

My father's family did just that.

When he was just eight years old, after the death of his own father, his family took the long boat ride to Ellis Island and the *land of the free.*

Perhaps the inscription found on the *Statue of Liberty* gave hope to these strangers in a strange land:

---

18 Fariña R. Been So Long It Looks Like Up to Me. Penguin Classics; 1966.

"Give me your tired, your poor,
Your huddled masses yearning to breathe free,
The wretched refuse of your teeming shore.
Send these, the homeless, tempest-tossed to me.
I lift my lamp beside the golden door."[19]

The intent of this statue was to provide hope for the American people after the assassination of President Lincoln. It served as a beacon not only for the multitudes overlooked within its shores but also for the huddled masses that would come.

We don't need a new and improved anthem for the disadvantaged within our nation. We just need to, once again, set a "...lamp beside the golden door."[19]

WE JUST NEED TO, ONCE AGAIN, SET A "...LAMP BESIDE THE GOLDEN DOOR."

We don't need a new *Declaration of Independence*. We just need to re-believe the original truth in Sacramento and throughout America. We need to acknowledge and affirm the original American Declaration: *"We hold these truths to be self-evident, that all men are created equal, that they are endowed by their Creator with certain unalienable Rights, that among these are Life, Liberty and the pursuit of Happiness."*

My father's first job in his new nation, at 11 years of age, was as a shoeshine boy in Brooklyn, New York. Eventually, he earned the titles: lawyer, judge, leader within the Italian community, a Congressman for five-terms, and a New York State Supreme Court Justice prior to his death at the age of 61 in 1966.

The Congressional Record documents a speech by Congressman Eugene Keogh in 1954 about my father:

"The first day he was in Congress Representative Anfuso, who had previously served as special assistant to the Commissioner of Immigration and Naturalization Service, introduced a bill to improve the immigration laws and to admit 34,000 aliens of Italian nationality unable to enter the United States during the war years. Because of the inequities of the McCarran-Walter immigration bill, he spoke several times on the floor of the House in opposition to that bill, pointing out its discriminatory and racist features and the injustices it contains. Even after he left

19 Lazarus E. "The New Colossus".

Congress at the end of 1952, Anfuso continued his fight against the McCarran-Walter Immigration Act in the hope of amending it to make it more liberal. He became chairman of the National Committee To Amend the McCarran Act and thus continued his efforts to eliminate those features, which are discriminatory against all races and nationality groups."[20]

You would have thought these attainments should have given him a sense a peace and accomplishment, but without the tranquility that comes from knowing Jesus, my father would die frustrated, having never grasped some unreachable rung of achievement. Only Jesus can set captive souls free.[21]

With my father's busy life in politics and the fact that my twin brother and I were born just as he was elected to his first term in Congress, we were shuffled out of the house as quickly as possible. Living in oppressive boarding schools from eleven to seventeen years old fueled my resentment and feelings of abandonment. I now realize this pain had a negative impact on my view of my Italian ancestry.

On my "Journey To Mosaic" with leaders from an assortment of ethnicities, which I will share about later in this book, I wept bitterly realizing for the first time that my hatred of my father had racial ramifications: ironically, only toward those of my own ethnic background. In our discussions, I realized that children of racial minorities at times form negative attitudes toward their own ancestry because of the peer pressures placed upon them. I was sadly no exception. Now, many years later, I have been healed of paternal resentments and one hope to see my father again in Heaven.

I AM NOT INVISIBLE

"The end of life is not to be happy, nor to achieve pleasure and avoid pain, but to do the will of God, come what may."

—*Dr. Martin Luther King Jr.*

No one wants to be invisible. We all desire to be seen, to have value, to be known for who we really are. Sadly, many minorities

---

20 Representative Anfuso (NY). Congressional Record 100 (June 21, 1951) p.911.
21 Luke 4:18

feel overlooked. Their concerns are ignored. Their lives are marginalized. They seem invisible. Oftentimes, the "white" majority, the dominant race, is the recipient of much privilege. It's the way it is, but not the way it should be.

If we carefully examine our own life experience, most of us have felt invisible at one time or another. Remembering our invisible moments will help us understand and empathize with those who live invisible lives.

It would take many years after his death, when I was 17, before I would connect the dots that my father in some way knew me. This momentary glimpse was contained in the only sentence I am aware he ever wrote about who he thought I was. But, before I say more, let me give it some context.

My father had some notable accomplishments. During World War II, when the Allies were preparing to reoccupy the European Continent, my father served in the OSS (Office of Strategic Services), the predecessor of the CIA (Central Intelligence Agency). Being Sicilian, he embarked on a secret mission to 1Sicily to enlist the Mafia's support of the Allied invasion.

I AM A FLAWED MAN DESPERATELY IN NEED OF A GRACIOUS SAVIOR TO RESCUE ME AND AN ALL WISE LORD TO RULE OVER MY SOUL AND SPIRIT.

After the war, when Communists gained a strong chance of winning the national election in Italy, he organized a letter writing campaign in which Italian-Americans wrote their relatives imploring them to vote against communism.

For leading this effort, he was knighted by Pope Pius XII.

On the framed picture of their meeting, my father hand wrote, *"To Frank (me), whose benevolence will ingratiate the hearts of many."* I wasn't invisible. He did see me.

For those few words I will always be grateful.

But no matter what my father did or didn't do, I am responsible for my own responses to the challenges in my life.

I am unable to present myself, or my fellow believers, as more whole than we really are. This would make me no better than the Pharisees of old. My only honest option is to acknowledge the obvious: I am a flawed man desperately in need of a gracious Savior to rescue me and an all wise Lord to rule over my soul and spirit. In order for this to happen, I must turn myself in daily, living a transparent life that embarrasses and costs me the most. I must do all I can to undo the false premise that, as a person born into a majority race, I am in some way more special than the minorities I am called to serve.

The ground is level at the cross. I must kneel at the feet of Jesus and find both forgiveness and strength to resist saying shallow, parroting words that cost me nothing. He gave His all, and so must I. He loved all people well, and so must I.

GOD IS A MOVING TARGET

"To be a Christian without prayer is no more possible than to be alive without breathing."[22]

—*Dr. Martin Luther King Jr.*

God is a moving target.

Either we move with Him, or we're left behind.

Jesus said, *"Whoever is not with me is against me, and whoever does not gather with me scatters."*[23]

The greatest joy in my life is flowing with God, moving with my Creator, letting Him lead me in the dance called life, trusting Him so completely that I never question where He's taking me or what He's doing.

I don't want to trust an airplane pilot more than I trust God—to ever believe that I know what's best for my life. I never have, and never will. The Bible says, "Commit everything you do to the Lord. Trust him, and he will help you."[24]

As the psalmist wrote, "Protect me, for I am devoted to you. Save me, for I serve you and trust you. You are my God."[25]

FROM SNOWFLAKES TO SUNFLOWERS, ELEPHANTS TO ANTS, PENGUINS TO PEOPLE, GOD'S CREATION IS AMAZING. EVERY RACE OF PEOPLE IS EQUALLY EXCEPTIONAL.

22 Sweeting G. Talking It Over. Moody Publishers; 1979.
23 Luke 11:23, NIV
24 Psalm 37:5, NLT
25 Psalm 86:2, NLT

Everything God created is remarkable, exceptional and one-of-a-kind. From snowflakes to sunflowers, elephants to ants, penguins to people, God's creation is amazing. Every race of people is equally exceptional. Their flavors permeate the Earth. Sure, we are flawed humanity, each bankrupt without a relationship with our Creator. But if your race were the only ethnos in existence, Jesus would have died for you.

The devil tries to destroy life's extraordinariness, just like he destroyed his own. But don't give up the riches of Heaven for the counterfeit treasures of Earth. Jesus said, "...the kingdom of heaven is like a merchant seeking beautiful pearls, who, when he had found one pearl of great price, went and sold all that he had and bought it." [26]

I used to read this and think, "I need to give God my whole heart in order to get the pearl of great price...Jesus."

Now I realize that God is the merchant and we are His pearls. He gave everything He had for us, even His life, so that we can spend eternity with Him.

Perhaps one of the residual benefits of residing in racially diverse Sacramento is having a role in fulfilling the Great Commission. "...this gospel of the kingdom will be preached in all the world as a witness to all the nations (Gr. ethnos), and then the end will come."[27] Ethnos in this verse refers to the entire human family.

You can be sure that God has targeted Sacramento. Trust Him to introduce you to someone of a different race than your own—someone who is hungry to experience Jesus.

Remember, God's vision is always more encompassing than our own. It usually involves transformation of our personal relationship, our family, our community and culture and beyond.

Hmm? Maybe God's plan for a fully revived Sacramento is designed to impact not just America, but the whole Earth.

26 Matthew 13:45–46, NKJV

27 Matthew 24:14, NKJV

VISITING MT. RUSHMORE BUT NEVER SEEING IT

"There is nothing more dangerous than to build a society with a large segment of people in that society who feel that they have no stake in it; who feel that that have nothing to lose. People who have stake in their society, protect that society, but when they don't have it, they unconsciously want to destroy it."

—Dr. Martin Luther King Jr.

At the end of the summer of 1970, I traveled west through Canada with a few friends in a van. We saw the Canadian Rockies, the Grand Teton Mountain Range in Wyoming, and on our way back, we went east across the U.S. into the Black Hills of South Dakota. There we continued to Mount Rushmore National Memorial, the granite mountain chiseled with faces of Presidents George Washington, Thomas Jefferson, Theodore Roosevelt and Abraham Lincoln.

While walking from the parking lot to this historic site, I encountered a Native American group from the Lakota (Sioux tribe) who were passionately professing their right to reclaim the Black Hills. They shared how this land was sacred to the Lakota and other Plains Indians long before it was exploited during the gold rush of the 1870s. Lakota ancestors had been deliberately killed and driven from land, treaty-promised to them in perpetuity. Their viewpoint was that the Black Hills was stolen and should be returned to the Lakota.

I was so captivated by their appeals for justice that I stood listening while my friends continued down the path to Mount Rushmore. When they returned, nearly an hour later, I realized my opportunity to see the memorial was over. I had traveled thousands of miles to a remote place to view something I had always wanted to see and now was driving away having been only a few hundred yards from beholding its majesty.

Ironically, my thoughts were not about what I had missed, but what I had just heard. It grieved me to stand by and watch those with broken hearts. I had just spent two summers, while in college, working with a federal government program called "Upward Bound," and living with underprivileged, primarily African-American, high school students from some of the toughest neighborhoods in northern New Jersey. Having heard their stories over and over again, my heart was ripe to receive a fresh appeal from others whose lives had also been devalued.

UNTIL I CARE FOR WHAT GOD CARES FOR, I CAN'T LIVE THE LIFE HE INTENDED.

Forty-five years later, I have still never seen Mount Rushmore, and will likely never do so, but as I reflect back upon that day, I am more fascinated by my willingness as a young man to empathize with the cry of a displaced people, than to do something that would have merely pleased me. For whatever reason, even as an atheist, God had hardwired me to care about the needs of others.

Is it any accident that each of us has been created in the image and likeness of the God who is love...that we love when He loves, care when He cares, and even ache when He aches?

This begs a further question: Will I turn a blind eye to what God wants me to see and a deaf ear to the cries He wants me to hear?

Though I can't do everything, I can always do something. Even Jesus didn't do everything, but He always did something even if it was just to pray and wait on His Father.

Until I care for what God cares for, I can't live the life He intended.

In order for us to do this, we will miss some things: some entertainment, some relaxation, and some lesser adventures, in order to do what we were made to do. The good must defer to the best if we are to be who we are created to be.

SOFT-MINDED MEN

"A nation or civilization that continues to produce soft-minded men purchases its own spiritual death on the installment plan."
—Dr. Martin Luther King Jr.

There's a syndrome that most two-year-olds experience. It's called, "You exist to bless me." Perhaps that's why it's called the "terrible two's." As parents, we know that part of the process of successfully raising children is to transition them from being *"natural-born takers"* into *"supernatural givers."*

There's no learning process in *"taking."*
We're all born *"master-takers."*
We're all born *"soft-minded."*

We have all been given many blessings from God, not just for our indulgence, but so that we may share the blessing with others. And the only way we can experience this greatest fulfillment in life is to learn how to give. Sadly, some adults' attitudes resemble the terrible two's. Their lives become self-absorbed time warps—thinking God exists to bless them.

Though God *is* a blessing to me, He doesn't exist to bless me. Though America *is* a blessing to me, it doesn't exist to bless me.

Teaching us to give is not God's way of equally distributing resources. It's God's way of raising children.

Frankly, human nature succumbs to the worthless; we tend to seek what lasts for a moment and ignore the priceless, that which God created to remain forever.

John Wesley said it well: *"We should only value things by the price they shall gain in eternity."* Everything we see with our natural eyes is temporary, lasting but a few moments compared to eternity, while all that is eternal is invisible and accessed only by faith. Invisible faith gives us the victory to overcome the seductions in this world.[28]

Genuine *"...faith is being sure of what we hope for, being convinced of what we do not see."*[29] For only by faith in Jesus

---

Christ's death and resurrection are we able to receive not just everlasting life, but access to the abundant life Jesus promised right here on Earth.

At some point we have to make the decision: Do we want to spend our lives as a patient or doctor?

Do we want to live in the receiving line or the giving line?

Strong-minded men and women want to live in the giving line.

They want to see God transform their lives and community more than they want to receive what pleases them.

> IF WE SEE OUR LIVES FROM GOD'S PERSPECTIVE, AT THE END OF THE DAY, WE'LL REALIZE THAT NONE OF US HAVE BEEN SHORT-CHANGED. ALL OF US HAVE BEEN LAVISHLY OVERPAID.

Strong-minded, fully submitted followers of Jesus, turn their world upside down. They are the true next-wave that will restore the true identity and destiny of Sacramento.

At times, all of us are patients needing to receive. But, we are never more like our
Creator than when we give and care for others.

We have all been given many blessings from God. The Bible says, *"...He gives to all life, and breath, and all things..."*[30]

If we see our lives from God's perspective, at the end of the day, we'll realize that none of us have been short-changed. All of us have been lavishly overpaid.

Each of us has a blessed life!

But few acknowledge their God-given blessings.

It takes faith to trust God—to take Him at His Word. When we stand before Him and see how pure His heart is, we will at last realize He wanted to bless us all along.

How much time have we wasted doubting His promises?

Don't spend your life in the receiving line when Jesus promised joy in the giving line. Hold your hands up with gratitude and enjoy living.

---

29 Hebrews 11:1, NET
30 Acts 17:25, KJV

It's been rightfully said, *"The surest way to be happy is to seek happiness for others."*[31]

What causes the dis—ease in our lives?

What leaves us most unsettled?

Being loyal to everything that has to do with self!

Ours is the generation of a million options, each costing nothing. Effortless, temporary, shallow fulfillment at our fingertips! We surf the illusion without breaking a sweat, making a commitment, or being loyal to anything but ourselves. It pre-conditions and hard-wires us for self-absorption, cherishing what appears to benefit "me" the most.

The only hope for breaking this independent spirit and cycle of entitlement is embracing a pure dependence upon God alone. Since no one knows you better than God, only He can satisfy the inner longings He placed inside you.

For "...you are complete in Him," and in Him alone.[32]

If you're a follower of Jesus, think back to one minute before you gave your life to Him.

Did God love you then?

Was He smiling or frowning?

Did He suddenly have a cosmic epiphany and realize He was head over heels in love with you? No! God loved you as much one minute before you received Jesus, as He did one minute after. He is not just a God of love, He's a God in love. God is so excited about the life He has given you, even your greatest challenges, He'll settle for nothing less than you loving it too.

So how do you learn to love your life? You'll love your life when you know God is always pleased and never disappointed; not with everything you do, but with everything you are. "God demonstrates His own love toward us, in that while we were still sinners, Christ died for us."[33]

When God thinks of you, is He sad or glad?

---

31   Dr. Martin Luther King Jr.
32   Colossians 2:10, NKJV
33   Romans 5:8, NKJV

God may be saddened over what you do, but He's never disappointed in you as His unique creation. God is not disillusioned with you because He had no illusions about you to begin with.

How can you surprise a God who sees past, present and future simultaneously?

He lives in a perfect place of complete understanding of your past and present, with an absolute hope for your future.

How can you disappoint a God who is all knowing and ever in your favor?

GOD IS NOT DISILLUSIONED WITH YOU BECAUSE HE HAD NO ILLUSIONS ABOUT YOU TO BEGIN WITH.

The psalmist describes God's thoughts toward us so clearly, *"How precious also are Your thoughts to me, O God! How great is the sum of them! If I should count them, they would be more in number than the sand..."*[34]

This verse makes it clear: God's infinite thoughts toward you are precious.

WHAT REALLY LASTS?

"I believe that unarmed truth and unconditional love will have the final word in reality. This is why right, temporarily defeated, is stronger than evil triumphant."

—Dr. Martin Luther King Jr.

Everyone wants to be attractive.

But do you want to be attractive for a moment or forever?

Most people choose the 15-minute option.

Not too long ago, the *Biography Channel* regularly featured lives of people who obtained genuine accomplishments. Now it primarily highlights celebrities.

Many people confuse fame with honor.

Madonna is famous.

Mother Teresa is honored.

---

34 Psalm 139:17, NKJV

Newspaper editor Horace Greeley once wrote, *"Fame is a vapor. Popularity is an accident and money takes wings. The only thing that endures is character. And the only thing worth honoring is character."*

Nero was once the Roman Emperor: the most famous man of his day. At the same time, Paul the Apostle was an obscure Jewish Christian leader who wrote a few letters. Virtually no one had heard of Paul, while everybody knew about Nero. How ironic that, two thousand years later, we name our sons Paul, and our dogs Nero.

You've probably experienced pleasures in life that satisfy... at least for a short time. You've eaten, drunk, smoked, seen and touched. But, like me, I'm sure you've found that your natural senses never truly fulfilled you. Only supernatural and eternal pleasures can do that.

Why should we give our hearts to someone or something that merely lasts for our brief lifespan here on Earth?

A human lifespan is a drop of water in the ocean of time.

Jesus advised, *"Don't store up treasures here on earth, where moths eat them and rust destroys them, and where thieves break in and steal. Store your treasures in heaven, where moths and rust cannot destroy, and thieves do not break in and steal."*[35]

What eternal treasures has God given you to help bring unity to all ethnicities in Sacramento?

WHY SHOULD WE GIVE OUR HEARTS TO SOMEONE OR SOMETHING THAT MERELY LASTS FOR OUR BRIEF LIFESPAN HERE ON EARTH?

CALIFORNIA AND SLAVERY

"If the inexpressible cruelties of slavery could not stop us, the opposition we now face will surely fail. We will win our freedom because the sacred heritage of our nation and the eternal will of God are embodied in our echoing demands."

—Dr. Martin Luther King Jr. *(Letter from a Birmingham Jail, 1963)*

Few possibilities spark greater excitement than the chance of getting rich quick! Not surprisingly, when gold was discovered in California in 1848, thousands scrambled to the Sierra foothills hoping to gain their fortune.

What most found was far less thrilling!

A young man from South Carolina, after spending three years in Sacramento, wrote: "California has a barbarous civilization, licentious morals, crude manners, and inclement climate... No one here can be successful unless he assimilates himself with the people. He must carouse with the villains, attend Sunday horse races, and adapt himself to depravity."

This was the atmosphere that greeted one of Sacramento's first pastors, Wm. Grove Deal, a medical doctor who became the fledgling city's first chaplain.

Soon cholera would strike, killing ten to fifteen percent of Sacramento's inhabitants. Within a few years, one in four would die from floods, fires or disease. With such a desperate need to bury the dead and comfort the living, local pastors came, accepting the challenge. While many fled the outbreaks of disease, a handful of ministers remained, placing the lives of their own families in peril.

In a short time, Sacramento grew to over 300,000 residents. Natural calamities gave way to unnatural behaviors. It was said that, "Gambling, prostitution, drunkenness, disorderly conduct, and lawlessness abounded."

These few courageous pastors met the multitudes arriving daily on ships, gathering them under oak trees by the docks of the "River of the Blessed Sacrament." It was there they shared the good news of God's love in an area which came to be known as "The Grove." The desperation of Sacramento's first citizens was so great, these founding pastors endeavored to meet both the natural and spiritual needs of those who often arrived sick, debilitated, and penniless.

It was here they advocated for the ill-treated Chinese immigrants. One pastor, Martin Briggs, courageously stood against outright prejudice. It was said of him: "When a wave of barbarism swept over the Coast and the Chinese were mobbed and churches were burned for the crime of teaching them the Gospel, his clarion voice was heard above the storm in defense of the oppressed race."[36]

In 1851, when outsiders lobbied for California to become a slave state, once again, Pastor Briggs spoke against the injustice and mistreatment of blacks. Pastors stood for what was right, even though it cost them dearly.

In addition to Sacramento's founding pastors who opposed slavery, John Fremont, the first U.S. civilian Governor of California and its first U.S. Senator, also refused to lent his support.

His story is quite extraordinary!

Fremont, a California pioneer totally devoted to the Bible, could memorize up to 300 scriptures in one day. American trailblazer Kit Carson said of Fremont, "...he suffered with his men undergoing the severest of hardships...I say without fear of contradiction, that none but him could have surmounted and succeeded through as many difficult services as he did."[37]

---

36 Sibole ES. First United Methodist Church — 135 Anniversary Publication. Sacramento: River City Lithography; 1973.
37 Col Carson C. 1856. Retrieved from: http://www.longcamp.com/kit.html on August 10, 2011.

"In 1856, he (Fremont) was the Republican nominee for president of United States. He was first offered the Democratic ticket for president, which was considered a shoo-in, but he would have had to compromise his anti-slavery principles and other political ethics, so he and (his wife) Jessie declined the offer."[38]

Each of us inherits values passed down from previous generations worth preserving while others are best discarded. As followers of Jesus, we have been entrusted with an immeasurable treasury of God's Word and even church history.

What responsibility do we have to retain the integrity of our godly heritage?

What distinctions have descended from Sacramento's past that are vital for her future?

Now it is our turn to mine the spiritual riches of our Christ-like ancestors, the reservoirs of those who have gone before us.

It is our turn to represent Jesus well!

SACRAMENTO'S RACIAL HISTORY

"Injustice anywhere is a threat to justice everywhere. We are caught in an inescapable network of mutuality, tied in a single garment of destiny. Whatever affects one directly, affects all indirectly."
(Letter from a Birmingham Jail, 1963)

—*Dr. Martin Luther King Jr.*

Because the lure for gold was so strong, it was recorded that forty-six Baptist ministers came through The Grove between April and August 1849 but did not come to preach. Six pastors, however, did: Pastors Wm. Grove Deal (Methodist Episcopal Church), Joseph Benton (Pioneer Congregational Church), Osgood Church Wheeler (Baptist), Isaac Owen and Dr. Martin Briggs (Methodist Episcopal Church), and William Taylor.

"They were united in their belief that the Gospel message of love and forgiveness as found in the Bible and taught by all groups of Christians was needed above all else in California. These

---

38 Falany H. God, Gold & Glory. Outskirts Press, Inc.; 2010.

Sacramentans also believed that Christian beliefs should form the basis of action in all of life and Christian ethics should be the basis of civilization. To that end, they worked to establish schools, to set up printing presses, to agitate for just government, and to fight against what they considered to be immoral practices in the community ...a living out of one's Christian life, and all of the good causes were seen as going hand in hand with the gospel presentation."[39]

As the enticement to find gold established a settlement, Sacramento's founding pastors began advocating for the disenfranchised. Joseph Benton saw the injustice of what was happening and addressed this social evil from his pulpit, marrying his proclaimed faith with an issue of unjust treatment of the Chinese.

In Benton's words: *"In some way the Providence of God will bring it to pass, that California shall fully compensate for every mischief she has done – that there shall be an antidote for her poison – that for all the avarice, covetousness, and cold hearted miserliness of which she has been the occasion, she shall make ample returns of good; of good in driving away superstition, breaking down the walls of prejudice and dissipating the darkness that has so long veiled and confused the minds of men uninstructed and half-civilized."[40]*

The Chinese were not the only group that caught the attention of the early ministers. Even though California had entered the Union as a free state, racist sentiments and unfair treatment of Blacks infiltrated the region. At the risk of putting himself in personal and professional danger, Pastor Martin Briggs, once again, became an advocate for the Blacks settling in Sacramento. The intensity of this issue cannot be overlooked.

In 1851, Briggs found out that some Southern politicians were meeting in Wilmington, North Carolina with plans to induct California as a slave state. Specifically, their agenda included: the influx of a large number of slaves to the developing state, modifying California law to annul the Constitution, and introducing a constitutional clause to legalize slavery in California. It is not known specifically how Briggs found out about this back-

---

39 Neuenburg FH. Turning Their World Rightside-Up. The Witness of Sacramento Churches, 1849–1859. Berkeley, CA: Master of Theological Studies Project, New College Berkeley; 1986.

40 Benton J. California As She Was, As She Is, As She Is To Be. Thanksgiving Sermon delivered November 30, 1850. California Room, Sacramento, California.

room-deal, but he publically exposed it in the *California Christian Advocate* (Methodist periodical) that he founded.

Briggs used his pulpit to publically denounce the mistreatment Blacks endured and the politics attempting to make slavery legal. This not only got him into trouble with those from the opposing view, but also his own Methodist congregation presented him to the Official Methodist Board who passed a motion charging him to stay home with his local congregation instead of traveling about the state speaking out against the mistreatment and racism toward the Blacks.

No matter the threats, Briggs would not stop. He mounted his horse and traveled wherever needed to speak for Christian justice.

Inevitably, relationships developed across racial lines by these early church leaders with Blacks, Chinese, and other minority groups, which profoundly impacted the emerging Sacramento city.[41]

RACIAL PREJUDICE DURING BIBLICAL TIMES

"Hate is just as injurious to the hater as it is to the hated. Like an unchecked cancer, hate corrodes the personality and eats away its vital unity. Many of our inner conflicts are rooted in hate. This is why the psychiatrists say, "Love or perish." Hate is too great a burden to bear."

—*Dr. Martin Luther King Jr.*

During the time of Jesus, Samaritans were considered half-breeds, despised by both Jews and Romans. By intermarrying with foreigners and adopting their idolatrous practices, Samaritans embraced a religious mixture of Judaism and idolatry[42] thus ostracizing them from the Jews.

Being Jewish and from Galilee, Jesus experienced racial prejudice firsthand.

JESUS MADE A CONSCIOUS DECISION TO FACE THE PREJUDICE AROUND HIM. HE DELIBERATELY WENT THROUGH SAMARIA.

---

41 Research provided by Pastor Bret Widman, River Life Covenant Church, Sacramento.
42 2 Kings 17:26–28

He understood all too well how bigotry destroys the fabric of a society. Consequently, when He traveled from Judea back home to Galilee, Jesus made a conscious decision to face the prejudice around Him. He deliberately went through Samaria.

A direct route from Judea to Galilee was about 70 miles, or a two and a half day walk. But due to prejudice, many Jews chose not to go through Samaria. They traveled on a hot desert road from Jerusalem to Jericho up the Jordan Valley. They were willing to journey almost twice the distance on a hotter and more indirect road, than to mix with or even encounter Samaritans. Jesus cut through this narrow-minded thinking.

> *"He (Jesus) left Judea and departed again to Galilee. But He needed to go through Samaria. So He came to a city of Samaria, which is called Sychar, near the plot of ground that Jacob gave to his son Joseph. Now Jacob's well was there."[43]*

Jacob's well was an historic spot. At the foot of Mount Gerizim, it was one half mile west of the village of Sychar, where the Patriarch Joseph's bones were buried. It was Joseph who modeled forgiveness to those who hated him: the brothers who sold him into slavery, Potiphar's wife who falsely accused him and sent him to prison for seven years, Pharaoh's chief cup-bearer who forgot about Joseph even after he had been restored to his position.

Jesus meant to re-dig a well of forgiveness.

Jesus talked with a *woman* at Jacob's well who, in addition to being a Samaritan, lived a promiscuous life.

> *"Jesus said to her, 'You have well said, "I have no husband," for you have had five husbands, and the one whom you now have is not your husband...'"[44]*

The disciples were appalled that Jesus was even talking with a woman:

> *"And at this point His disciples came, and they marveled that He talked with a woman; yet no one said, 'What do You seek?' or, 'Why are You talking with her?'"*

43 John 4:3–6a, NKJV
44 John 17b–18a, NKJV

In this chapter of John, we see Jesus overcoming three dimensions of prejudice: Racial, Gender and Religious. Because He was a friend of sinners,[45] Jesus had a heart to build bridges and heal breaches, *"...many of the Samaritans of that city believed in Him..."*[46]

It's been said that, "Your friend is the person who knows all about you and still likes you."[47]

Does anyone know us better than God?

Does anyone love us more than God?

"For God did not send His Son into the world to condemn the world, but that the world through Him might be saved."[48]

What better way to demonstrate God's love than by building bridges and healing breaches between those Jesus came to save?[49]

THE WOMAN AT THE WELL'S OLD TESTAMENT COUNTERPART

"Love is the only force capable of transforming an enemy to a friend."
—Dr. Martin Luther King Jr.

An Old Testament counterpart to the Woman at the Well was a Canaanite woman from Jericho, Rahab the Harlot. She, too, had to overcome three dimensions of prejudice: Racial, Gender and Religious, but is now listed in the genealogy of Jesus, separated by 31 generations.

Jericho was the first city the Israelites conquered in their Promised Land. It came, not by might, nor by power, but by God's miraculous intervention. The Israelites obediently marched around Jericho over a seven-day period culminating as the walls of the city collapsed. Though all of the inhabitants of Jericho were killed, Rahab and her family were rescued having tied a scarlet thread to her window.

How open is God the Father to breaking Racial, Gender and

---

45 Matthew 11: 16–19, John 8: 1–11
46 John 4:39, NKJV
47 Elbert Hubard
48 John 3:17
49 Special thanks to Pastor Scott Hagan from Real Life Church in Sacramento who provided some of the insights mentioned above.

Religious prejudice? He chose a Canaanite prostitute to be a part of the lineage of His beloved Son. "...The Spirit and the bride say...whosoever will let him take the water of life freely."[50]

The "whosoever will may come" has never been rescinded.

The scarlet thread that Rahab tied outside her window, and that spared her life, is still available to all.[51]

The end time harvest will spread throughout the whole Earth until "...this gospel of the kingdom will be preached in all the world as a witness to all the nations, and then the end will come." [52]

God's ultimate intention is expressed so clearly in these verses "...if there is any encouragement in Christ, any comfort from love, any participation in the Spirit, any affection and sympathy, complete my joy by being of the same mind, having the same love, being in full accord and of one mind. Do nothing from selfish ambition or conceit, but in humility count others more significant than yourselves. Let each of you look not only to his own interests, but also to the interests of others. Have this mind among yourselves, which is yours in Christ Jesus..."[53]

Think about this.

The Israelites willingly accepted Rahab into their fold, which became a healing balm for her ignorance.

We feed the racial divide by harshly judging other people because we disagree with their views. How can you win someone who believes something different than you do? Start by not allowing a belief to characterize the person. The Bible says, "... and such were some of you..." but you're not like that anymore.

We damage our influence by making another feel ungodly due to his or her ignorance or lack of understanding.

God is far more a bridge builder than a wall maker.

We must be no less.

Our efforts to love people from all ethnicities well will provide the groundwork for a mighty move of God in Sacramento.

---

50 Revelation 22:17
51 Joshua 2:15, 18, 21
52 Matthew 24:14, NKJV
53 Philippians 2:1–5, ESV

CHAPTER 5

LIVING IN AMERICA'S MOST RACIALLY DIVERSE CITY

*"We must learn to live together as brothers
or perish together as fools."*

—Dr. Martin Luther King Jr.

Living in our city and our nation is both a great privilege and responsibility. It should humble us, not make us proud.

Famously known as a prisoner of war under the Nazis, Corrie ten Boom was once asked if it was difficult for her to remain humble. Her reply was simple, *"When Jesus rode into Jerusalem on Palm Sunday, on the back of a donkey, and everyone was waving palm branches and throwing garments on the road, and singing praises. Do you think that for one moment the donkey thought any of that was for him?"*

Everything we have has been given to us. Therefore we have no reason to glory in ourselves. Truly humble people understand how undeserving they are of their blessings. The Bible says, *"By humility and the fear of the LORD are riches and honor and life."*[54]

The branch bearing the most fruit is bent lowest to the ground.

> **THE BRANCH BEARING THE MOST FRUIT IS BENT LOWEST TO THE GROUND.**

At times our branches bend because of fruit, at other times because of adversity. Either way, God bestows humility as an outcome and grace as a reward.

So how does one humbly live in America's most racially diverse city while actively reaching out to neighbors? The cross-pollination of races can either be seen as a stumbling block or a stepping-stone, a pathway to something new and historic, or a roadblock creating pain and division.

Sacramento's racial tapestry is perhaps her most exquisite gift to America! Our diversity can either be seen as a privileged glimpse into the inevitable future of our nation, or a burdensome challenge that is more a liability than an asset.

I see Sacramento's potential as gold waiting to be discovered!

Though we have all been hurt and hurt others, those who survive the planet without becoming emotionally jaded are the ones who really win the game of life.

So how do humble people do that?

The Bible says, *"Watch out that no poisonous root of bitterness grows up to trouble you, corrupting many."*[55]

Whenever we are unable to process hurts in a healthy way, they become festering wounds, contaminating not just our lives, but also even those closest to us. Over time we create alternate realities, a new north. That's why the Bible says, *"Above all else, guard your heart, for it affects everything you do."*[56]

Do you have an offense? Has someone hurt you, or have you been wounded by a failed expectation?

It's been said that an expectation is an offense waiting to happen. Think about that for a moment. What offense do you have? Now trace it back to an unfulfilled expectation. Someone didn't act the way you hoped, or something didn't happen the way you expected.

The Bible says, *"My soul, wait silently for God alone, for my expectation is from Him."*[57] I've wasted too much time waiting for my will to be done or for someone else to act the way I thought best. Now I'm just waiting on God. He is worth waiting for and has never failed me.

---

55 Hebrews 12:15, NLT
56 Proverbs 4:23, NLT
57 Psalm 62:5, NKJV

How would you describe yourself: a wounded victim or a scarred warrior?

How we respond to life's body-slams makes all of the difference in how fruitful we are in life. The Message Bible paraphrases Paul's commendation to the Corinthians after challenging them in a previous letter. *"Now I'm glad—not that you were upset, but that you were jarred into turning things around. You let the distress bring you to God, not drive you from him. The result was all gain, no loss. Distress that drives us to God does that. It turns us around. It gets us back in the way of salvation. We never regret that kind of pain."*[58]

HOW WOULD YOU DESCRIBE YOURSELF: A WOUNDED VICTIM OR A SCARRED WARRIOR?

Don't be a victim; rejoice in each struggle that brings you closer to God. Be encouraged. God wants to make you a hero! That's always been his intent. Why? Because that's what He did with His Son, the first fruits of a new creation. [59]

He allowed Him to seem the victim by dying for our sins so He could ultimately become a Hero by conquering sin and death. His heroic obedience to the Father rescued the entire human race. We have the power to live this same victorious life only when we are plugged into the source of our eternal health. For then we become "...more than conquerors through Him who loved us."[60]

Once you've been hurt, it's harder to trust. And since all of us have been hurt, it's hard for us to trust anyone...even God. Lack of trust may be evidenced not just in 60-year-olds, but sad to say, in 6-year-olds as well. Perhaps the greatest test in life is an ability to trust after a wound. That's why the Bible says, "...be kind to each other, tenderhearted, forgiving one another, just as God through Christ has forgiven you."[61]

While being hurt by others is inevitable, Jesus compels us to follow His example of forgiveness, saying, he who has been forgiven little loves little; but he who has been forgiven much, loves much.[62] We realize the extent of God's love when we

---

58 2 Corinthians 7:9–10, MSG
59 Colossians 1:15
60 Romans 8:37, NKJV
61 Ephesians 4:32, NLT
62 Luke 7:47

receive and then offer others the same forgiveness we have been freely given.

One of the remarkable bridge-building miracles of unity and forgiveness that has been taking place in Sacramento since 2007 is the quarterly City Pastors Fellowship Luncheon. Started by a humble couple who pastor a small church, Don and Christa Proctor, there is no agenda at these gatherings except fellowship, encouragement, and prayer. Their generosity in initially underwriting these luncheons provoked all of us to step up and give. Now hundreds attend and various churches take turns hosting as their church members cater the luncheons, which has been a great blessing to all.

Selfless generosity will leave you speechless, change your heart, and make an unforgettable memory!

I have a niece who went on a mission trip to Poland. After staying and ministering to a humble family there, as she was about to leave the country, her hosts wanted to give her something to express their appreciation.

What they did next was beyond her comprehension.

They took the only picture they had in their modest home off the wall and gave it to her. It was their most prized possession. She was stunned...overwhelmed with emotion. Giving what you don't need or want isn't giving at all. It's merely a garage sale. They had given her their best. It reminds us of Jesus, doesn't it? He gave His best for us...His very life. It's no wonder we feel best when we do the same.

Compared to people around the world, most Americans are rich.

Tell someone from Cuba or Haiti, "You're not rich!" They don't risk their lives to get here on rickety boats, across a treacherous ocean, because they're into yachting!

A few years ago, a pastor friend helped some Russian Christians immigrate to Sacramento. When he took them to a typical American supermarket, the family huddled in an aisle and said, with tears in their eyes, "Never in our wildest dreams did we ever think people could live like this."

Do you know what you have?

If so, do you appreciate it?

It's been said, "You'll never value what you'll receive if you can't appreciate what you already have."

When you and I live grateful, humble, forgiving lives, we're seeing life as God intended.

DON'T GIVE UP ON PEOPLE

"Life's most persistent and urgent question is,
'What are you doing for others?'"
—Dr. Martin Luther King Jr.

What do people see in us?

The Bible says, "...God made two great lights, the sun and the moon..."[63] To expand the meaning of this verse, think of Jesus like the sun, the greater light that doesn't reflect...He imparts. On the other hand, we are the lesser light, the moon, merely reflecting the light of the sun. We have no light within us!

Without God we reflect and impart nothing of eternal value. Yet Jesus encourages us, "You are the light of the world."[64] If Jesus is our Lord, then we are called to be a light in a world lost in darkness.

We may be the only light people ever see.

Perhaps what will reflect the most light is a willingness to repair the relational breaches in our lives? Are there relational breaches in your life that need repair?

> WE MAY BE THE ONLY LIGHT PEOPLE EVER SEE.

I've found that most people have them. I once met a man who shared that he hadn't seen his only son in twelve years. When I tried to comfort him, he shot back brashly, "It's his loss, not mine!" Sad! I found it revealing that he knew exactly how long it had been since he had spoken to his son.

Have you invented an imaginary reality to soothe an unbearable sadness? If you have, then take comfort in knowing God

---

63 Genesis 1:16a, NLT
64 Matthew 5:14, NLT

wants to repair your breaches, heal your divisions, and reconcile your relationships. The Bible calls Jesus the "repairer of the breach."[65] The Father sent Jesus to heal broken hearts,[66] and He has called each of us to be His "ministers of reconciliation."[67] I don't want to stop loving people because I know God will never stop loving me.

My heart goes out to every mother who has a breach in a relationship with her child. If that's you, please don't give up. I once read about a mother who prayed 60 years for her son to receive Jesus. One week before she died, she received a long distance phone call saying that he'd given his heart to Jesus.

My own mother prayed fervently for all of her children. I was especially lost. In 1971, as a vehement atheist, I would laugh at her as she prayed over her food. But she and God had the last laugh. Though I was thousands of miles away, and she hadn't seen me in nine months, I wandered into a little country church and received Jesus on Mother's Day. Immediately, I knew it was because of her prayers. Never stop praying for your children!

God is the original promise keeper. He is a God of covenant, who never makes a pledge He doesn't keep from now unto eternity. God is all about eternity! He makes promises! More importantly, He keeps promises! He always backs up His word, and doesn't quit. He doesn't give up on us. Ever!

Today, God wants to make a covenant with you because He loves you and because He wants to extend His love to Sacramento through you. A covenant based on who He is—love. God is love! Others may forsake us, but God never will! His love never fails! The Bible promises, "He is the faithful God who keeps His covenant for a thousand generations and lavishes His unfailing love on those who love Him and obey His commands."[68]

God pledges to impart His everlasting love.

All we have to do is receive it that we may freely reflect it.

---

65   Isaiah 58:12

66   Luke 4:18

67   2 Corinthians 5:18

68   Deuteronomy 7:9, NLT

THERE ARE NO SHORTCUTS...ONLY DETOURS

*"The first question which the priest and the Levite asked was:
'If I stop to help this man, what will happen to me?'
But...the Good Samaritan reversed the question:
'If I do not stop to help this man, what will happen to him?'"*
—Dr. Martin Luther King Jr.

In the 1840's, an overly ambitious man named Lansford Hasting said he knew of a shortcut to California. He dreamed of making California a territory he could rule. So in the spring of 1846, 87 men, women, and children left Springfield, Illinois. This ill-fated group became known as the Donner Party.

The journey would have lasted four months if they had stayed on the proven trail. But instead Hasting chose a route he had never traversed before. His way proved to be far more treacherous and 125 miles longer. Instead of four months, it took a year, and 41 of the 87 members died horrible deaths along the way.

To add to their difficulties, the Donner Party encountered the worst winter in the history of the Sierra Nevada Mountains. Many of those facing starvation were reduced to cannibalizing their dead companions. Years later, one of the survivors referred to what she had learned from the ordeal, saying, "In life, there are no shortcuts."

One of the greatest incentives for resisting wrongdoing is knowing the absolute fact that you will be caught; severe consequences await you on the other side, and you will regret it.

GOD NEVER EATS LEFTOVERS, AND HE DOESN'T WATCH RERUNS. NEITHER SHOULD WE!

Moses thought no one was watching when he made his wrong decision, "...he looked this way and that way, and when he saw no one, he killed the Egyptian and hid him in the sand."[69] Just because Moses saw no one, didn't mean he hadn't been seen. He then fled for his life and lived in a desert for 40 years. The Book of Hebrews says, "Nothing in all creation is hidden from God's sight. Everything is uncovered and laid bare before the eyes of him to

---

69 Exodus 2:12, NKJV

whom we must give account."[70] Truly "The fear of the Lord is the beginning of wisdom."[71]

So in order to avoid detours, dead ends and distractions, what does a healthy Christian life look like?

It will always look unfamiliar and unexpected.

If you and I keep experiencing the same challenges and adventures in our Christian life, it probably means we are going in a circle.

God never eats leftovers, and He doesn't watch reruns. Neither should we!

Those who truly follow Him can expect the unexpected.

The Old Testament records the children of Israel soon forgetting the miseries of Egypt. They would have exchanged the freedom and hope of their future for the familiar slavery of their past. Isn't that just like us? As in the case of Lot's wife, at times we look back even though we know there's nothing there.

Consider Paul the Apostle's advice. He said, "...one thing I do: forgetting what is behind and straining toward what is ahead."[72]

Forget what you cannot change, and look forward to a future only a loving, all-powerful Father could imagine.

Imagine what God's all-powerful imagination has in store for Sacramento if her people were to catch His vision. As one of her citizens, avoid the detour and fix your eyes ahead.

---

70 Hebrews 4:13, NIV
71 Proverbs 9:10, NIV
72 Philippians 3:13, NIV

WHEN ARE YOU GOING TO COME TO US?

*"Not only will we have to repent for the sins of bad people;
but we also will have to repent for the appalling
silence of good people."*

—Dr. Martin Luther King Jr.

Why are the things that are most valuable always hidden?

Gold...diamonds...oil...even true love.

It's the same with God. He hides what is most valuable to Him so that it might become precious to us.

The Bible says, "It is the glory of God to conceal things, but the glory of kings is to search things out."[73] and, "You will seek me and find me. When you seek me with all your heart..."[74] Jesus added, "Ask, and it will be given to you; seek, and you will find; knock, and it will be opened to you."[75]

We appreciate what costs us much.

He stretches our spiritual muscles to mold us into people that look like Him. Jesus shared the same principle in this parable: "The kingdom of heaven is like treasure hidden in a field, which someone found and hid; then in his joy he goes and sells all that he has and buys that field."[76]

---

73 Proverbs 25:2, ESV
74 Jeremiah 29:11, ESV
75 Matthew 7:7, NKJV
76 Matthew 13:44, NKJV

Are we willing to find what God has concealed?

The gold hidden in Sacramento's foothills provided a natural path to a supernatural destiny. Its discovery opened the door to the most prosperous future of any state in the Union.

What gold is yet to be found in the relational treasures God has hidden in our region? We all need a do-over, a second chance to discover what we have missed.

I once went on a prayer retreat with pastors from the Sacramento region. One of them, Bishop Sherwood Carthen, the man to whom this book is dedicated, was a leading African-American pastor. He was greatly esteemed by leaders in both the church community and secular culture.

THE GOLD HIDDEN IN SACRAMENTO'S FOOTHILLS PROVIDED A NATURAL PATH TO A SUPERNATURAL DESTINY. ITS DISCOVERY OPENED THE DOOR TO THE MOST PROSPEROUS FUTURE OF ANY STATE IN THE UNION.

One afternoon, a very candid discussion took place about race realities between Sherwood and another highly respected white pastor. I stayed out of the discussion until I felt they were at an impasse. They both loved and respected each other, but somehow they just weren't connecting. Finally, with great emotion, I said to Sherwood, "My brother, what do you want us to do? We'll do whatever you ask."

He expressed that there seemed to be little effort, amongst many church leaders, to build bridges of understanding and healing. He then added a knockout sentence.

"The road from me to you is the same distance as from you to me. We are always coming to you. When are you going to come to us?"

The words were piercing to all of us! With a second chance to hear Sherwood's heart, he was finally heard.

"THE ROAD FROM ME TO YOU IS THE SAME DISTANCE AS FROM YOU TO ME. WE ARE ALWAYS COMING TO YOU. WHEN ARE YOU GOING TO COME TO US?"

Further discussion of specifics brought about City Pastor's Fellowship involvement in future events connecting us with the African-American community, one of which is the annual "MLK – March For The Dream" which takes place every January. Within a year, hundreds of pastors, leaders and believers from throughout our region marched in support with thousands of our African-American brothers and sisters. I believe in 2015 there will be thousands more and increased involvement from regional pastors and churches.

All of this was a result of that one awkward, yet vulnerable conversation. Which leads me to share a vitally important conviction. The church and the culture really need leaders: faithful, godly, servant leaders...willing to ask and hear the right questions.

What's the #1 reason there are so few leaders?

One word: FEAR!

The fear of changing and the fear of leading!

The fear of changing will keep us from hearing those who have first hand experiences that we do not. If we can hear them, their life journey is designed to broaden our understanding and expand our hearts. As a white man, I cannot grasp what it is like to be a minority. So if I am to become all things to all men, I must come a humble learner. God longs to bring the privileged and powerful to serve the under-served, not as rescuers, but as seekers of truth that will set others and even ourselves free.

Likewise, the fear of leading isn't new either. Everyone fights it. From feeble Lot, who lost his family's respect and became incapable of leading them, to outspoken Peter, who denied Jesus and wept bitterly.

At times, we have to hate what we have become in order to embrace what we are meant to be.

> AT TIMES, WE HAVE TO HATE WHAT WE HAVE BECOME IN ORDER TO EMBRACE WHAT WE ARE MEANT TO BE.

It will take courage to be a rescuer in this age of rampant numbness! It will take even more courage to first reject numbness in myself. The Bible says, "God has not given us a spirit of fear and timidity, but of power, love, and self-discipline."[77]

Fifty people "95 and older" were asked, "If you had to live your life all over again, what would you do differently?" One of their primary responses was, "I'd take more risks!"

---

77 2 Timothy 1:7, NKJV

Hmm? How revealing! But not surprising!

If faith is one of the things that pleases God most, is it any wonder that acting in faith would please us as well?

One Sunday, after speaking in a church, I went to have lunch with the pastor in a crowded restaurant. When he asked me to pray over the food, the Lord immediately prompted me to invite the entire restaurant to pray as well.

Was I surprised? No...shocked! But I knew it was God.

Without processing it for too long so as not to become paralyzed, I stood up and, with a loud voice and a big smile, I said to the 50 people who could hear me, "Could I have your attention, please?"

The busy room went completely silent in about 10 seconds.

I continued, "You know we're having such a wonderful time here with family and friends in this great restaurant; why don't we just take a moment and thank God for this beautiful day?" I then bowed my head and offered a brief, uplifting prayer before sitting down.

What happened next was even more surprising.

I looked over at the pastor I was with and found that he had passed out in his food.

Ha! No, but that's what I thought would have happened.

But God had a better plan.

Throughout the meal people began to come over and thank me— even waitresses. It's funny how just obeying God, in seemingly risky moments, is simply the best thing we can do.

We are created in God's image and likeness. We should, therefore, take more risks! Not foolish, impetuous risks, but embracing the Spirit-led opportunities God has written into His perfect script for us.

He wants to raise up a fearless leader in you.

The Bible says, "...we are God's masterpiece. He has created us anew in Christ Jesus, so we can do the good things he planned for us long ago."[78]

The future of Sacramento belongs to fearless leaders who will stare down uncertainty and welcome the unknown as a dear friend.

THEY NEED TO GET OVER IT

"Forgiveness is not an occasional act, it's a constant attitude."

—Dr. Martin Luther King Jr.

After speaking in a weekend service, I received an anonymous note from a man complaining about my Valentine's weekend sermon. He had wanted me to exhort the women as strongly as I did the men and was upset I had not.

I still have no interest in following his advice.

It's my deep conviction that men need to be men, becoming the leaders of their families. I, likewise, believe it's time for single men to treat the women around them with honor, leading by example, which means laying down our lives for the women in our lives, just as Christ laid down His life for the Church. I've counseled enough men who refuse to lay down their lives for their brides. Enough!

We live in a culture that encourages men to be predators and not protectors, to use women rather than honor them and treat them with respect.

Men, lay down your lives for the beautiful women around you!

In a similar way, I believe it is the responsibility of the dominant culture to honor the less-dominant minorities around them.

We are clear that those who have suffered generational mistreatment through hundreds of years of abuse and degra-dation *cannot just get over it.* As there has been generational humiliation and debasement, now there must be generational affirmation and healing. The fears of many minorities have not been unfounded. "White mythology" often conceals their true history because what actually happened is just too painful to admit. But when I sincerely acknowledge the pain and loss of those who have experienced such generational trauma, I am more like the publican who admitted his sin than the delusional Pharisees who chanted, "I thank you, God, that I am not a sinner like everyone else."

Before some of you turn off and check out from hearing what I am trying to say, let me draw on excerpts from Dr. Martin Luther King's historic, *"Letter From a Birmingham Jail."* Dr. King had led months of lengthy protests in one of the South's most racially unjust cities, Birmingham, Alabama. When he was arrested for non-violent, civil disobedience, he penned one of the great documents in American history on April 16, 1963.

Here are some excerpts from this letter written to white clergymen in Birmingham who wanted Dr. King and others to wait to take action, or perhaps even "get over it."

> *"Injustice anywhere is a threat to justice everywhere. We are caught in an inescapable network of mutuality, tied in a single garment of destiny. Whatever affects one directly, affects all indirectly."*

> *"We had no alternative except to prepare for direct action, whereby we would present our very bodies as a means of laying our case before the conscience of the local and the national community."*

> *"...it is an historical fact that privileged groups seldom give up their privileges voluntarily."*

> *"...justice too long delayed is justice denied."*

> *"Perhaps it is easy for those who have never felt the stinging darts of segregation to say, 'Wait.' But when you have seen vicious mobs lynch your mothers and fathers at will and drown your sisters and brothers at whim; when you have seen hate filled policemen curse, kick and even kill your black brothers and sisters; when you see the vast majority of your twenty million Negro brothers smothering in an airtight cage of poverty in the midst of an affluent society; when you suddenly find your tongue twisted and your speech stammering as you seek to explain to your six year old daughter why she can't go to the public amusement park that has just been advertised on television, and see*

tears welling up in her eyes when she is told that Funtown is closed to colored children, and see ominous clouds of inferiority beginning to form in her little mental sky, and see her beginning to distort her personality by developing an unconscious bitterness toward white people; when you have to concoct an answer for a five year old son who is asking: 'Daddy, why do white people treat colored people so mean?'; when you take a cross county drive and find it necessary to sleep night after night in the uncomfortable corners of your automobile because no motel will accept you; when you are humiliated day in and day out by nagging signs reading 'white' and 'colored'; when your first name becomes 'nigger,' your middle name becomes 'boy' (however old you are) and your last name becomes 'John,' and your wife and mother are never given the respected title 'Mrs.'; when you are harried by day and haunted by night by the fact that you are a Negro, living constantly at tiptoe stance, never quite knowing what to expect next, and are plagued with inner fears and outer resentments; when you are forever fighting a degenerating sense of 'nobodiness'— then you will understand why we find it difficult to wait. There comes a time when the cup of endurance runs over, and men are no longer willing to be plunged into the abyss of despair. I hope, sirs, you can understand our legitimate and unavoidable impatience."

Have things improved since this tragic time? Absolutely!

But is there no vestige of racial injustice in our society?

We have come a long way, and are headed in the right direction, but more work needs to be done.

More hearts need to be changed. More attitudes enlightened.

Simultaneously, we realize that some in the next generation of African-Americans *are* significantly *over it.* They have close friends of all ethnicities and cultures. Likewise there are many young whites who have grown up colorblind to friendships and even embrace marrying someone of another race or adopting a child of a different color or culture.

THE NEXT GENERATION IS NOT HARDWIRED FOR BIGOTRY. THEY ARE HEART-WIRED FOR HARMONY.

The next generation is not hardwired for bigotry.

They are heart-wired for harmony.

The Bible says, "...a little child will lead them."[79] I have seen this in the next generation of young people of all ethnicities. They are ready and able to lead. I know this is true and have experienced it firsthand, over and over again.

Here's a story that will illustrate this conviction.

When my daughter Deborah was about six years old, we went for a walk in the Oregon woods. But it wasn't until it was getting dark that I realized we were lost. Sadly, it doesn't take much for me to get lost.

So I said, "Deborah, I think we're lost!"

She said, "I know how to get us back."

I looked at her for a very long time. She was six years old, three-foot nothing! She could barely tie her shoes.

So I said, "Are you absolutely sure, Deborah?" She said, "Yep!"

And so, as it was getting really dark, she took me by the hand and led me out of those "dark, scary woods."

It was an affirmation of a significant revelation: *the next generation will be leading us in Sacramento before we know it, and it will be a good thing.*

Today my twin daughters are mothers to seven children, as well as ministers, leading many.

CHAPTER 7

BELIEVING FOR THE IMPOSSIBLE

"So the question is not whether we will be extremists, but what kind of extremists we will be. Will we be extremists for hate or for love? Will we be extremists for the preservation of injustice or for the extension of justice? In that dramatic scene on Calvary's hill three men were crucified. We must never forget that all three were crucified for the same crime—the crime of extremism. Two were extremists for immorality, and thus fell below their environment. The other, Jesus Christ, was an extremist for love, truth and goodness, and thereby rose above his environment."

—*Dr. Martin Luther King Jr.*

Do you feel completely incapable of fulfilling what God is asking you to do?

Wonderful! It's probably taken years for God to get you there.

This is a healthy place to be: having no confidence in your own ability—realizing if you rely on your own efforts you cannot be who God has asked you to be nor do what He's asked you to do.

Your only hope is in God!

This is reality for every human being, though few know it and fewer still live it. When David was living in a cave as an outcast, he had little choice but to fully trust in God. But when he became a successful king, he counted his army and relied on his own strength.[80] This merely brought a curse.

Rejoice in your weakness, it is your only hope of true success.

One of the greatest Christians who ever lived, Paul the Apostle, knew it. He wrote, *"For when I am weak, then I am strong."*[81]

Why would you ever attempt to do the impossible?

For only one reason: you were absolutely certain that God asked you to meet an impossible need!

Impossibilities provoked Jesus to live an impossible life, and they provoke me as well. Jesus said, *"...with God all things are possible."*[82]

What impossible life is Jesus asking you to live?

What would you do if you knew in the deepest part of your being that God was committed to helping you complete a particular endeavor?

What if God were asking you to be the first in your family to step across racial boundaries?

> WHY WOULD YOU EVER ATTEMPT TO DO THE IMPOSSIBLE? FOR ONLY ONE REASON: YOU WERE ABSOLUTELY CERTAIN THAT GOD ASKED YOU TO MEET AN IMPOSSIBLE NEED!

Not something that you invented or would ever initiate, but what you're absolutely persuaded is on God's heart. It may appear highly unlikely, or even impossible, but no matter. If an all-powerful God would fulfill this specific hope or dream, what would you believe for?

The Bible says, "Faith is the confidence that what we hope for will actually happen; it gives us assurance about things we cannot see. By faith we understand that the entire universe was formed at God's command, that what we now see did not come from anything that can be seen."[83]

Every day we must stake our claim on God's ability to fulfill His promises.

There is so much pain in our world. So many suffer injustices, battle feelings of insignificance, have little hope for resources and a future.

Only God knows how much!

---

81 2 Corinthians 12:10, ESV
82 Matthew 19:26, ESV
83 Hebrews 11:1,3, NLT

And He cares!

Even at this moment, He wants to help us believe for the impossible!

The Bible says, *"because Jesus lives forever...he is able...to save those who come to God through him. He lives forever to intercede with God on their behalf."*[84]

It promises that Jesus *"...understands our weaknesses, for he faced all of the same testing we do, yet he did not sin. So let us come boldly to the throne of our gracious God. There we will receive his mercy, and we will find grace to help us when we need it most."*[85]

Jesus will always meet you at your point of greatest need!

Do you feel like you've had a slow start to stepping out in faith?

One of the greatest followers of God, Abraham, did as well. Early in his life he disobeyed God, lied to rulers, and deceived others. His life and future was a roll of the dice. But then the lights came on. God turned up the heat, forged his mettle and wielded a man of integrity, honor, and faith.

The Bible says, "It was by faith that Abraham obeyed when God called him to leave home and go to another land that God would give him as his inheritance. He went without knowing where he was going."[86]

You don't have to know where you are going in order to follow God. All you have to do is rest and trust that He knows.

> YOU DON'T HAVE TO KNOW WHERE YOU ARE GOING IN ORDER TO FOLLOW GOD. ALL YOU HAVE TO DO IS REST AND TRUST THAT HE KNOWS.

FIRST IT IS IMPOSSIBLE

"...only when it is dark enough, can you see the stars."

—*Dr. Martin Luther King Jr.*

Don't be surprised if God asks you to do something you've never done before.

---

84 Hebrews 7:24–25, NLT

85 Hebrews 4:15–16, NLT

86 Hebrews 11:8, NLT

Noah stepped out in faith, even though he hadn't seen many of the things set before him.

God said, *"Noah, build Me an ark."*

Noah responded, "God, what's an ark?"

God answered, *"It's the big boat you're going to need when the flood comes."*

Noah again replied, *"God, what's a flood?"*

God explained, *"It's going to rain so much that the whole earth is going to be covered with water."*

One more time Noah exclaimed, *"God, by the way, what's rain?"*

Noah then obediently built the ark. How's that for blind faith? Could the same faith help end racism in America?

Some would say it could not.

Others believe as I do: Sacramento, America's most ethnically diverse city, is positioned to lead our nation into racial harmony.

Once again, it may seem a farfetched possibility.

That's why I close every email I send people with this quote *"First it is impossible. Then it is difficult. Then it is done."*

It is a phrase coined by Hudson Taylor, the great missionary to China. He faced innumerable difficulties pioneering a Christian mission in ancient China, which included burying both his young wife and three of his children. Yet he prevailed in building a bridge of hope across a racial divide and is honored as the man who brought the gospel to the planet's largest population.

Jesus spoke of the impossible like this, "With men this is impossible, but with God all things are possible.'"[87]

One reality we, as true followers of Jesus, must continually realize is that we are most useful to God when we feel most useless.

> ONE REALITY WE, AS TRUE FOLLOWERS OF JESUS, MUST CONTINUALLY REALIZE IS THAT WE ARE MOST USEFUL TO GOD WHEN WE FEEL MOST USELESS.

---

87 Matthew 19:26, NKJV

When God said to Paul, "My grace is all you need. My power works best in weakness." Paul then wisely responded, "So now I am glad to boast about my weaknesses, so that the power of Christ can work through me."[88]

Think of the Bible's greatest comebacks. From God's perspective, aged Abraham and Sarah were prime candidates for having a baby. Exiled, disgraced and well past his prime, Moses was the perfect choice to deliver the Israelites. Childless and desperate Hannah was perfectly suited to become the mother of the great prophet Samuel. The Kingdom of God is often counter-intuitive, most clearly seen in God as the man, Jesus.

George Washington Carver, the brilliant African-American scientist, once asked God to tell him about the universe. According to Carver, the Lord replied, "George, the universe is just too big for you to understand. Suppose you let Me take care of that?" Humbled by this response, Carver replied, "Lord, how about a peanut?" The Lord said, "Now, George, that's something your own size. Go to work on it and I'll help you."

By the time he was done studying the peanut, he had discovered over 300 products. He believed it was all because he asked God's advice. All of us need God's wisdom, that's why James wrote, "If any of you lacks wisdom, let him ask God, who gives generously to all..."[89] and later he said, "you don't have what you want because you don't ask God for it."[90]

NEVER CHOOSE THE EASY WAY

"There comes a time when one must take the position that is neither safe nor politic nor popular, but he must do it because conscience tells him it is right."

—*Dr. Martin Luther King Jr.*

A famous football player's discipline ethic provides an excellent example of the level of integrity followers of Jesus should adopt. He said, "When I'm working out alone, I expect every bit as much from myself as I do when coaches or teammates or

88 2 Corinthians 12:9, NLT
89 James 1:5, ESV
90 James 4:2, NLT

workout partners are watching. No shortcuts. No cheating. No manipulating. No rationalizing. I know that nobody's watching. I know that no one would ever know… I want to know I have done everything I needed to do to prepare myself… I can allow no shortcuts, not even in private."

WOW! That sounds like a great goal for each of us.

Who I am in private is who I am!

WHO I AM IN PRIVATE IS WHO I AM!

The Bible says, "…the day is coming when God, through Christ Jesus, will judge everyone's secret life."[91]

Never choose the easy way, unless God chooses it for you.

I love this annoying quote, "If you're not living on the edge you're taking up too much space."[92]

For me an edgeless day is a wasted day. A thoughtless moment is spiritual senility and a misuse of God's grace.

There is nothing more awkward and edgy than being completely vulnerable and transparent.

I want to live fully awake, absolutely honest about who I am and am not, wholly connected to my fully awake, fully revealed Creator.

God plans tests for each of us to purge indolence; every one designed to awaken and draw us closer to Him. The Bible says that when Moses had come of age he refused to be called the son of Pharaoh's daughter.

Why?

Was he a fool?

He could have been counted amongst Egypt's rulers, given his own gold coffin, and maybe even had a pyramid named after him, but Moses refused to follow the decadence of the Egyptian culture. He knew that you couldn't be a true follower of God and simultaneously follow the world. He knew there is no shorter, easier way to God's best.

91 Romans 2:16, NLT
92 Stephen Hunt

Though Moses never made it to the Promised Land, the Book of Revelation says that in eternity they will sing the song of Moses and the song of the Lamb.

Paul said, *"I'm not trying to win the approval of people, but of God."*[93]

Obedience is not always an easy way; it does require absolute integrity.

The Bible teaches that obedience precedes healing, answered prayer, and righteousness.

OBEDIENCE IS NOT ALWAYS AN EASY WAY; IT DOES REQUIRE ABSOLUTE INTEGRITY.

After the children of Israel were delivered from the Egyptians and miraculously passed through the Red Sea, the Lord gave them a promise, "I am the Lord who heals you." The prerequisite for this magnificent statement is found in the previous verse. "If you diligently heed the voice of the Lord your God and do what is right in His sight, give ear to His commandments and keep all His statutes, I will put none of the diseases on you which I brought on the Egyptians."[94]

Though we may not fully comprehend it or see it while on Earth, obeying God will eventually bring blessing, healing, and deliverance.

Would you believe me it I told you that many Christians are practical atheists?

They believe in God, but for all practical purposes, they don't really believe He will do anything supernatural in their lives or the lives of others; supernatural things like healing, deliverance, or even victory over temptation. Even still, God's Word and promises are true! It is impossible for Him to lie.[95]

The way to see God's promises fulfilled in your life and for Sacramento is through obedience. The way to see a city that looks like Heaven is to yield completely and ultimately to God.

---

93 Galatians 1:12, NLT
94 Exodus 15:26, NKJV
95 Hebrews 6:18

Here are two scriptures worth believing when your only option seems difficult.

> *Jesus said, "The Spirit of the Lord is on me, because he has...sent me to proclaim freedom for the prisoners and recovery of sight for the blind, to set the oppressed free..."*[96]

> *"God is faithful, and he will not let you be tempted beyond your ability, but with the temptation he will also provide the way of escape, that you may be able to endure it."*[97]

Though everyone dies, few people die obediently believing. Even fewer die obediently believing for the impossible.

96 Luke 4:18, NIV
97 1 Corinthians 10:13, ESV

CHAPTER 8

THE ONE THING YOU COULD DO

"The early Christians rejoiced when they were deemed worthy to suffer for what they believed. In those days the Church was not merely a thermometer that recorded the ideas and principles of popular opinion; it was a thermostat that transformed the mores of society." (Letter from a Birmingham Jail, 1963)

—Dr. Martin Luther King Jr.

Part of the reason I volunteered to live with needy inner city African-American young people almost immediately after Dr. King's death was because I had done so little to follow the principles he espoused so powerfully.

Though there was nothing I could do to bring Dr. King back or end racism in America, I made a decision to at least do something. Nevertheless, at 19 years old, I battled penitent feelings of "too little, too late."

No one leaves the planet without, at one point, wishing they could go back in time...return to a moment of weakness, a poor decision, words that should not have been said and actions we wish we'd done or never done. We're all stricken by the same affliction.

It's called regret.

Only God can free us from its clutches. He sent His Son Jesus to die for our sins; even for every mistake we've ever made. God's Word promises, *"If we confess our sins, he is faithful and just to forgive us our sins and to cleanse us from all unrighteousness."*[98]

One of Heaven's great attractions is the promise of forever living without regret. *"He (God) will wipe away every tear from their eyes, and death shall be no more, neither shall there be mourning, nor crying, nor pain anymore, for the former things have passed away."*[99]

But for now we need to do two things:

First, forget, by following Paul the Apostle's advice. *"...one thing I do: forgetting what lies behind and straining forward to what lies ahead, I press on toward the goal for the prize of the upward call of God in Christ Jesus."*[100]

Secondly, obey the promptings of God's Spirit, reaching out to whomever, wherever, and whenever He leads.

During the Vietnam War, a Vietnamese child volunteered to give blood so that other children could live. When she was led into a room and asked to lie down on a table to give blood she began to cry. An Army nurse came over and, through an interpreter, asked if she was hurt. The little girl said, "No," but kept crying. Finally, the nurse asked the interpreter to find out why the girl was sobbing. After talking to her for a few minutes the interpreter told the American nurse that when the little girl was asked to give blood, she thought the nurse meant: Was she willing to give all of her blood so someone else could live?

The little girl was willing to lay down her life for total strangers.

Is there any greater love than that?

Growing up in New York City, my twin brother and I would always run to catch the subway Express Train. Why? Because we knew it was, by far, the fastest way to get to where we wanted to go. Local trains stopped at every stop...way too slow.

In the same way, I've found that God's will is the express train to living a fulfilled life...the best and fastest way to experience the life I'd want, if I knew every option.

> GOD'S WILL IS THE EXPRESS TRAIN TO LIVING A FULFILLED LIFE...THE BEST AND FASTEST WAY TO EXPERIENCE THE LIFE I'D WANT, IF I KNEW EVERY OPTION.

---

99 Revelation 21:4, ESV
100 Philippians 3:13–14, ESV

God will never ask you to do something He wouldn't do, or be something He wouldn't be. Whatever request He asks of us is not just for our good, it's the best possible option. *"Trust in the Lord with all your heart...Seek His will in all you do, and He'll show you which path to take."*[101]

All of us need a life and death operation, an open-heart surgery, giving God entrance into the center of our being.

Once there, He will help you forget, obey, live without regrets and ride the fast track to His best. He will do this not only for you but through you so that others can know His best.

"I will give you a new heart, and a new spirit I will put within you. And I will remove the heart of stone from your flesh and give you a heart of flesh."[102]

A new heart and a new spirit may be the one thing you need for the sake of Sacramento.

LITTLE THINGS THAT CHANGED THE WORLD

"Whatever your life's work is, do it well. A man should do his job so well that the living, the dead, and the unborn could do it no better."

—Dr. Martin Luther King Jr.

A man was attracted to a rock he found in a stream. He brought it home and, for a long time, he made it a doorstop in his house. One day a geologist visited him and saw the rock. He identified it as pure gold. It was the largest piece of gold ever found east of the Mississippi River. It was a doorstop in someone's home. Considered insignificant! Worthless!

He didn't know what he had!

Do you know what you have?

Do you really believe you are insignificant to God? Worthless?

Nothing could be further from the truth.

---

101 Proverbs 3:5–6, NLT
102 Ezekiel 36:26, ESV

The truth is what the Bible teaches, "For we are God's master-piece. He has created us anew in Christ Jesus, so we can do the good things he planned for us long ago."[103]

I once was waiting at a store for tires to be put on my car when an elderly couple, severely hunched over with walkers, came in. My first thought about them was pity. But when we sat and chatted, I found that Laverne and Betty Bartz, 84 and 83 years old, and married 64 years, were quite extraordinary.

Three times a week for the last two years, they drive through Starbucks and give a gospel tract with a $5 gift certificate to the person in the car behind them. They've had numerous testimonies of people, even police officers, who felt their act of kindness was a kiss from God.

One tiny action can change a life.

An avalanche of tiny actions can change a city, even our city called to be a sacrament, something holy and unforgettable.

How about you? Has God rescued you? Are you grateful?

I know I am!

What tiny action of love could you do to liberate someone of a different nationality, race or language?

I will never forget how He released me from the depths of despair and set me on the path that leads to life. I will never forget those who reached across imaginary divides to love me well. They showed me Jesus and I have never been the same.

So what should we do if we've been saved? The psalmist provides some great advice, *"Has the Lord redeemed you? Then speak out! Tell others he has redeemed you from your enemies."*[104]

Every day people are sent our way who desperately need God. Some of them will look significantly different than we do, and yet God has prepared divine appointments for us.

---

103 Ephesians 2:10, NLT
104 Psalm 107:2, NLT

Frankly, I had very little in common with my spiritual father, my first pastor. But the differences were overshadowed by how visible God was in his life. He was the right person to guide my fledgling relationship with Jesus.

Jesus said, *"No one lights a lamp and then puts it under a basket. Instead, a lamp is placed on a stand, where it gives light to everyone in the house. In the same way, let your good deeds shine out for all to see, so that everyone will praise your heavenly Father."*[105]

In 1974, for a few months as a young Christian, I worked as a dishwasher in a casino in South Lake Tahoe, California. Because I was someone who could be trusted, my boss had me clean the gourmet kitchen, alone, all day long. One day, as I finished mopping my way out of the kitchen, I caught a strand from the mop on the back leg of a dishwasher. Initially, I shrugged it off thinking, "No one will notice. I'll get it tomorrow."

But as I walked the long corridors back to my locker, the Holy Spirit convicted me: "If you are not concerned about a string, one day you might not be concerned about a penny or a person." I went back and crawled under the dishwasher knowing I was working for the Lord and not man.

Now, decades later, I still believe God cares about little things, and so should I.

God cares about little things. It is He alone who holds every molecule in the Universe together.

God cares about every person in every race in the city of Sacramento, and He asks us to do the same.

Jesus said, "If you are faithful in little things, you will be faithful in large ones. But if you are dishonest in little things, you won't be honest with greater responsibilities. If you are untrustworthy about worldly wealth, who will trust you with the true riches of heaven? And if you are not faithful with other people's things, why should you be trusted with things of your own?"[106]

The answer is: you shouldn't be.

---

105 Matthew 5:15–16, NLT
106 Luke 16:10–12, NLT

The success of each of our lives will come down to being like Jesus, and that will always involve how we respond to the seemingly insignificant circumstances and seemingly unimportant people in our lives.

Is it any accident that, when a survey was conducted and people were asked what quality they would most desire in a spouse, and given the options of loving, affectionate, giving and faithful, more people chose faithful than all other options combined?

Why? Because faithfulness is the glue that keeps relationships together!

What would my wife had said to me if, on our wedding day, I vowed to be 99% faithful?

She would have said, "Take a hike!"

Likewise, who wants to follow a God who isn't faithful? No one!

The psalmist wrote this for sure when he wrote, "Your faithfulness endures to all generations..."[107], and "Trust in the LORD... feed on His faithfulness."[108]

Faithfulness literally means firmness.

It speaks of security, moral fidelity, stability, steadiness and truthfulness.

As trust is the attitude we most need when relating to an invisible God, knowing He is faithful will keep us secure in Him no matter what struggles we face.

I hold on to God's faithfulness, His firmness every day.

Being a Christian is a marathon; those who finish have one thing in common. They remained faithful! But since we are all at times faithless, the only Person who can keep us faithful is the only One who truly is faithful...God Himself. The Bible says, "If we are faithless, He remains faithful; He cannot deny Himself."[109]

He cannot deny who He created us to be.

---

107 Psalm 119:90, NKJV
108 Psalm 119:90, NKJV
109 2 Timothy 2:13, NKJV

Our *unfaithfulness* can't dissolve God's faithfulness.

His *faithfulness* continually draws us back to Him. If we'll let it, God's faithfulness is designed to transform us. It is one of the benefits of knowing Him.

The fruit of God's Spirit is faithfulness.[110]

What does faithfulness to God look like?

I believe when we commit to doing nothing without Him, then He can trust us to do His will.

WELCOME TO AMERICA!

"In some not too distant tomorrow the radiant stars of love and brotherhood will shine over our great nation with all their scintillating beauty."

—Dr. Martin Luther King Jr.

The secret of making people feel valued is to honor them.

A bi-lingual pastor in Los Angeles has seen his church grow to many thousands by doing just that. Whenever he meets a Mexican-American he asks them, "Has anyone welcomed you to America since you've been here?" Invariably they will say, "No!" Then, with a big smile, and total sincerity, he says, "I'm so sorry that hasn't happened yet. Let me be the first to say to you, 'Welcome to America! We're glad you're here!" The response to these heartfelt words is often shocking. Smiles come to faces, tears to eyes.

They've finally been welcomed to their new home.

They've been honored.

The Message Bible says, "Treat the foreigner the same as a native. Love him like one of your own. Remember that you were once foreigners..."[111]

---

110 Galatians 5:23
111 Leviticus 19:34

One of my favorite verses about honoring others is, "Do not forget to entertain strangers, for by so doing some people have entertained angels without knowing it."[112]

Why does God highlight the stranger, the unfamiliar one, the outsider, and the out-of-my-comfort zone person?

Because everyone is important to God!

We're all created in His image and likeness—given precious deposits of His character, personality and gifting. Therefore everyone should be important to us—treated with respect. Since God believes in honoring, it should be one of our values as well. The Bible says, *"Honor all people."*[113]

This word *"honor"* literally means, *"to prize, to revere, to value."* Often prejudice comes from lack of honor and respect. We devalue someone else for our own benefit. Honoring and respecting others would completely eliminate prejudice from the planet.

However, though we honor others, it should never replace the honor of God. And we should never focus on receiving honor for ourselves. In that way, honor is like chewing gum.

Enjoy honor briefly, but don't swallow it.

WHY I USE THE TERM "AFRICAN-AMERICANS"

"We must speak with all the humility that is appropriate to our limited vision, but we must speak."

—Dr. Martin Luther King Jr.

A good friend of mine who pastors a significantly multi-racial church in a southern state once asked me why I used the term "African-American" and not "black" when referring to people of color. It was a valid question which I understood as I myself had made the transition from "black" to the present description, "African-American."

---

112 Hebrews 13:2, ESV
113 1 Peter 2:17, NKJV

He wondered if I was in some way pandering to the "politically-correct" thought police by using the more cumbersome phrase. I shared with him that I had made the verbal transition after asking some of the African-American leaders I respected which description they recommended I use. Their rationale can be summed up this way: use whatever term the broadest number of people consider acceptable. Frankly, some of my friends would rather be called "black" and others "African-American."

I will say whatever is most appropriate to honor the person or audience I am addressing.

Some of the verses in the Bible that encourage me to have this sensitive attitude are, "...I have made myself a servant to all, that I might win more of them...To the weak I became weak, that I might win the weak. I have become all things to all people, that by all means I might save some. I do it all for the sake of the gospel, that I may share with them in its blessings."[114]

A similar word adjustment has been made in the U.S. with the terms *Asian vs. Oriental.*

Asian is now acceptable whereas *Oriental* is not.

Oriental is used to refer to *things* (e.g. food, souvenirs, rugs, etc.).

Asian people are not *things.*

Consequently, in the U.S., people are *not* referred to as *Oriental.*

Laying down our lives for others should be seen as an opportunity and not a burden. Jesus said, "Blessed are the meek, for they will inherit the earth."[115] This word meek is most often seen as being humble or gentle but also implies flexibility.

It costs me nothing to honor others by referring to them in a manner they consider most appropriate. What inconvenience am I caused by a respectful address? Furthermore what purpose does any unkind comment serve?

Consider "Miriam and Aaron (who) spoke against Moses because of the Cushite woman whom he (Moses) had married..." Moses, whom the Bible refers to as "...very meek, more (meek)

---

than all people who were on the face of the earth." He married a black woman for which his family ridiculed him. There is no record of Moses' defense or retaliation to their criticisms. Likely he quietly let it settle trusting in God's plan. Sure enough, God responded to their prejudice and struck Miriam with leprosy. "... Miriam was leprous, like snow."

May we each become meek enough to honor, with words, actions, and grace those we are called to love and serve in our divinely diverse city, Sacramento.

BEING INVISIBLE IS A GIFT

"...you are what you are because of somebody else. You are what you are because of the grace of the Almighty God. He who seeks to find his ego will lose it. But he who loses his ego in some great cause, some great purpose, some great ideal, some great loyalty, he who discovers, somehow, that he stands where he stands because of the forces of history and because of other individuals; he who discovers that he stands where he stands because of the grace of God, finds himself."

—Dr. Martin Luther King Jr.

There are many qualities of God that we hope to emulate, but here's one that few consider: being invisible. The Spirit of God reminded me of this quality once and invited me to become more like Him... more invisible. It continues to provide a wonderful filter for my life.

I now regularly ask myself these questions:

1. Is it necessary for me to be the person being seen?
2. Is there someone more suited to model a particular dimension that I could recognize, affirm and draw out?
3. Where can someone else increase and I decrease?
4. Is there an opportunity to acknowledge and honor the call and gifting of someone else?

---

116 Matthew 6:3, ESV
117 Philippians 2:3–4, ESV

Each of these questions has a biblical allusion:

1. Jesus said, "But when you give to the needy, do not let your left hand know what your right hand is doing..."[116]

2. Paul wrote, "...in humility count others more significant than yourselves. Let each of you look not only to his own interests, but also to the interests of others."[117]

> HOW CAN I REPRESENT JESUS WELL TODAY AND YET REMAIN INVISIBLE?

3. John the Baptist said, "He must increase, but I must decrease."[118]

4. Paul wrote, "Love one another with brotherly affection. Outdo one another in showing honor."[119]

As God resists the proud and gives grace to the humble, we can release the grace and power of God by making God and others more visible in our lives.

I call this a "Strategy of Humility."

It allows me to be intentional from the beginning in order to see God move, rather than being reactionary and inviting Him to bless what I am doing.

Here are some questions to ask in order to activate the "Strategy of Humility" and the grace and power of God:

*   What work does God want me to begin or join in order to bring Heaven to Earth?

*   Who is God drawing my attention to that he wants me to affirm and promote?

*   What is the biggest need I see, and who has the gifting and calling to meet that need that I could encourage?

*   If there were a move of God in the Sacramento region, what responsibility would I have?

"How can I represent Jesus well today and yet remain invisible?"

---

118 John 3:30, NKJV
119 Romans 12:10, ESV

CHAPTER 9

ONE FRIEND AT A TIME

"Love is understanding, redemptive goodwill for all men, so that you love everybody, because God loves them. You refuse to do anything that will defeat an individual, because you have agape in your soul. And here you come to the point that you love the individual who does the evil deed, while hating the deed that the person does. This is what Jesus means when he says, 'Love your enemy.' This is the way to do it. When the opportunity presents itself when you can defeat your enemy, you must not do it." [120]

—Dr. Martin Luther King Jr.

Imagine if learning to love were as simple as buying a software program when your heart was empty, or upgrading your "heart drive" when you needed more love. What if we could instantly wipe away past hurts, insecurities and resentments? Wouldn't that be nice? But learning to love just isn't that easy.

Actually, it takes a miracle to really love—a miracle only God can perform. Thankfully, it's one He not only wants to do in us, it's a miracle He began on the cross and perfectly completed in His resurrection. His sinless life, sacrificial death, and transforming resurrection give us the power to love even the "unlovable" as He loves—unconditionally and to forgive as He forgives. This pure kind of love will take a lifetime to learn, but it begins the moment we let Jesus become the Lord of our lives.

Would it surprise you if I told you that God the Father loves you as much as He loves Jesus? And not a bit less! Jesus said,

---

120 King, Jr ML. Loving Your Enemies. A Gift of Love: Sermons from Strength to Love and Other Preachings.

"I have loved you even as the Father has loved me. Remain in my love."[121]

WOW! If I'm as loved as Jesus, then God the Father is as pleased with me as He is with Jesus. Not with everything I do, but with everything I am. That was always His plan: to send Jesus to die for my sins so that I could be fully accepted by God. In Christ we are completely justified...just as if we've never sinned. The Bible says, "In Him (in Jesus) we have redemption through His blood, the forgiveness of sins, according to the riches of His grace."[122]

How I believe God sees me will determine how I see others.

Does God continually focus on what I'm not? Does God mean to inspire me with, "But you're not..." And then list all the differences between Him and me? Of course not! Imagine entering Heaven greeted by God's list of things He would have done on Earth, but I neglected.

HOW I BELIEVE GOD SEES ME WILL DETERMINE HOW I SEE OTHERS.

That actually sounds more like Hell than Heaven.

Likewise, if this was His approach on Earth, I doubt many of us would want to follow Him. It's the goodness of God that inspires us to change.[123] With kindness He drew us.[124] "Because of the Lord's great love we are not consumed..."[125]

How you see yourself will also affect how you view others. Do you believe you are beautiful to God...greatly loved and treasured? It's the doorway to experiencing the greatest joy in life. If we believe as God states, "Let Us make man in Our image, according to Our likeness..."[126] then we are each beautiful to God.

Certainly the God who made all that is beautiful on Earth must be beautiful Himself. If we say we're not beautiful, then we are assuming God isn't beautiful as well. The truth is, our identity rests in the fact that a beautiful God created us and loves us.

---

121 John 15:9, NLT
122 Ephesians 1:7, NKJV
123 Romans 2:4
124 Jeremiah 31:3
125 Lamentations 3:22
126 Genesis 1:26, NKJV

As beautiful as Jesus is, so is His spotless bride. In the Song of Solomon God says, "You are all fair, my love, and there is no spot in you."[127]

I can only give what I've received.

If I haven't been forgiven, I can offer little forgiveness.

If I don't love myself, I won't be able to unconditionally love others.

If I don't believe God gave His life for me, then I'll have no desire to give my life to Him.

It all relates to the Law of "Sowing and Reaping." God sows His love in me, so I can love other people. When Jesus died for my sins, He reaped what I had sown. You and I, as His followers, don't get what we deserve; thankfully, Jesus already did that... He took the punishment for us.

Here's a great goal: get as much good heavenly seed in the ground as possible. Your seed will always determine your harvest, whether good or bad, and we all will receive a harvest!

WHOEVER DIES WITH THE MOST HEAVENLY SEED IN THE GROUND WINS!

Whoever dies with the most heavenly seed in the ground wins!

Would you consider a farmer presumptuous to expect the land in which he's sown seed to bear fruit? Similarly, wouldn't it be absurd to expect a harvest from a piece of land into which you've sown nothing? All of us sow something and reap something. I believe it's fair to say, "You and I will reap exactly what we have sown." Embrace the challenges that come your way, and respond to them as you would a seed. Seeing them as appointments or disappointments is always the choice. Take some time to reflect each day on the seeds you're sowing.

In the gospels, a grateful woman broke a jar of very costly perfume and anointed Jesus.[128] Some of those present said indignantly, "Why this waste of perfume? It could have been sold for more than a year's wages and the money given to the

127 Song of Solomon 4:7, NKJV
128 Mark 14:3

poor."[129] Judging from the response of these disciples, you would have thought she had broken the jar over His head.

Can you imagine giving away a year's wages in one day, in one single action?

Hers was an incredibly sacrificial gesture.

That's why Jesus said, "Leave her alone. Why are you bothering her? She has done a beautiful thing to me... She did what she could."[130]

Her gracious action makes me ask the following question.

What is Jesus asking me to do for Him?

What seeds are waiting to be planted?

What stalks are waiting for harvest?

When a flock of crows invades a field of corn, the birds customarily station two sentries in a nearby tree to keep watch and warn the rest of any danger. Once there were two people who succeeded in sneaking up on a flock of crows and scaring them before the sentries had given warning. The birds burst into flight, immediately attacking and killing the two sentries who had failed to warn the flock. Only then did they fly away.[131]

Each of us is responsible for others and to others.

We are one another's life saving check and balance.

We are our brother's keeper!

If the greatest act of love is to lay down my life for others, then this responsibility must be the greatest seed I could ever sow.

God has put someone, most likely someone not like you, in your life to watch over. Through the beautiful things you will do for that person, the city of Sacramento will begin to look like Heaven.

129 Mark 14:4–5
130 Mark 14:6, 8
131 Tan PL. Encyclopedia of 7700 Illustrations. Rockville. Assurance Publishers, 1979.

LOVING THE LEAST

"Don't allow anybody to make you feel that you're nobody."
—Dr. Martin Luther King Jr.

Writer Tennessee Williams was once asked, *"What's the secret to happiness?"*

His misguided response was one word, "insensitivity."

In other words, don't let anyone or anything affect you enough to rob you of your happiness. Hmm? Is becoming completely insensitive to the world around you really the key to happiness?

I don't think so!

I like what Jesus said about happiness far better. If happiness does exist, He who created genuine happiness would certainly know how to find it. In Acts 20:35, the Amplified Bible quotes Jesus saying *"It is more blessed—makes one happier and more to be envied—to give than to receive."* Happiness is not getting all you can, it's learning to give all God asks. God's not trying to make your life livable, He wants to make it meaningful.

Meaningful equals *happiness.*

Let's talk about meaning.

TRUST BELIEVES GOD HAS ALL OF THE CLARITY WE'LL EVER NEED.

A man visited the House of the Dying in Calcutta, India to find out how to best spend the rest of his life. When he met Mother Teresa he asked her to pray for him. "What do you want me to pray for?" she responded. He then shared the most pressing burden on his heart, "Pray that I may have clarity." Mother Teresa answered him firmly, "No, I will not do that." Surprised, he asked her why. She told him, "Clarity is the last thing you are clinging to and must let go of." He countered by stating his admiration for the clarity she seemed to walk in. She laughed and said, "I have never had clarity; what I have always had is trust. So I will pray that you trust God."

Trust believes God has all of the clarity we'll ever need.

At one point, as a young Christian, I struggled with finding the will of God for my life. Because of a number of strong voices telling me what I should and shouldn't do, I was emotionally distraught about missing His will. In tears, I asked my pastor for advice. What he shared with me has guided my life through countless decisions over three decades.

He said, "Francis, it is impossible for you and I to miss God's will if we desperately want His will more than anything else."

Wow! What a word!

God, as a loving Father, will not fail to guide our lives into rich meaning. Without Him happiness simply cannot be found. Paul wrote, "I know whom I have believed and am persuaded that He is able to keep what I have committed to Him until that Day."[132]

LOVING YOUR ENEMIES

"...we shall never be true sons of our heavenly Father until we love our enemies and pray for those who persecute us."
Dr. Martin Luther King Jr.

Of all the categories of people we might consider unlovable, enemies might stand out. That's why Jesus shocked the world when He said, "You have heard that it was said, 'You shall love your neighbor and hate your enemy.' "But I say to you, love your enemies, bless those who curse you, do good to those who hate you, and pray for those who spitefully use you and persecute you, for if you love those who love you, what reward have you?"[133]

So, how do I learn to love unconditionally?

We must go to the source of unconditional love, a source that emanates from only one place, the heart of God. In the book of Jeremiah, God says, *"I have loved you with an everlasting love; therefore with loving-kindness I have drawn you."*[134]

What does that mean?

Something beyond your wildest dreams!

132 2 Timothy 1:12, NKJV
133 Matthew 5:43–45
134 Jeremiah 31:3, NKJV

God is saying, *"There's nothing you could ever do that would cause Me to stop loving you. There's nothing you could ever do to make Me love you more, and there's nothing you could ever do to make Me love you less. My love for you is everlasting, imperishable, unwavering."*

What could compare to receiving unconditional love?

One thing: unconditionally loving others!

Only Jesus can make that possible.

OUR "JOURNEY TO MOSAIC"

"We must work with determination to create a society, not where black men are superior and other men are inferior and vice versa, but a society in which all men will live together as brothers and respect the dignity and worth of human personality.

—Dr. Martin Luther King Jr.

In the summer of 2014, thirty regional Sacramento leaders went on a "Journey to Mosaic." J2M is a four-day experiential ethnic immersion bus trip through California. It explores historical and present-day injustices and challenges facing our multi-ethnic society. Participants process the issue of race "real time". They express hope of attaining breakthroughs so desperately needed. Bishop Sherwood Carthen called his J2M experience "life-changing." It was our thought as well.

The victories God desires require courage to enter uncharted territories, conquering lands presently occupied by the enemy of our souls. For this reason, specific individuals were invited for their leadership grace, diversity, and willingness to share honestly. J2M provided a safe conversation about race realities in the U.S. that affect how we live and minister. Our mission was to build bridges, heal breaches, and tear down walls that hinder us from finding the cure for this curse called "racism."

Our particular team included people from a rainbow of ethnicities: Persian, Palestinian, Latino, Asian, White, and African-American, men and women with a fire in their bellies for revival! We cried, laughed, hugged, loved, and shared our pain, hopes and guts freely. We met people from a variety of ethnicities along the way who shared their stories and those of their ancestors. We saw videos exploring a wide assortment of racial struggles that rocked our world, changed our paradigms, and unearthed our neatly filed away perceptions. We will never see one another and our respective races in the same way. God's heart for all people groups transformed us.

For information about J2M go to: http://pswc.org/resources/ J2M/

BEING RIGHT IS OVERRATED

"We must speak with all the humility that is appropriate to our limited vision, but we must speak."

—Dr. Martin Luther King Jr.

There's a revealing conversation in "The Great Divorce" by C.S. Lewis. It takes place in Heaven where one of the characters says to a spirit being: "'Everything I say or do is wrong, according to you.' 'But of course!' said the Spirit, shining with love and mirth so that my eyes were dazzled. 'That's what we all find when we reach this country. We've all been wrong! That's the great joke. There's no need to go on pretending one was right! After that we begin living.'"

What a profound statement!

Heaven's great joke is that there's no need to go on pretending or believing we are right.

Admit when we are wrong, and then begin to really live.

Being right is overrated!

Doing right is the main event.

Yet we all fail often. If we process our failures incorrectly, they will not produce the eternal fruit God intended.

Do you believe your mistakes have disqualified you?

If anyone could have thought that, it would have been the apostle Peter. He's a perfect example of someone who blew it, just like each of us, but God restored him. After denying the Lord three times, Peter thought he was disqualified.

How would it feel to desert your best friend in his greatest hour of need? Well, that's exactly how Peter must have felt. And that's why the angel, after Jesus rose from the dead, said, *"Go, tell His disciples--and Peter--that Jesus is going before you..."*[135]

...and Peter...

Jesus specifically mentions Peter because Peter would deem himself unworthy of the Lord's forgiveness. But God forgave Peter for his sins. He will forgive you, too.

One of the principal reasons people don't come to Jesus is because they can't differentiate between guilt and shame.

One leads to deliverance and life, the other to bondage and death. When we do something we know is wrong, it is normal for us to feel guilty...our God-given conscience has been activated. We feel convicted to change our behavior.

This is good and beneficial.

Shame, on the other hand, doesn't try to correct behavior; it assaults our very being and makes us believe the essence of who we are is flawed. The accuser throws his darts, and makes us feel worthless...broken...defective.

That's where Jesus found the woman at the well—smothered with shame. Jesus offered her a lifeline of hope; He conveyed the truth of her value. She then ran to tell everyone who had ever used, rejected or dismissed her exclaiming,

"I am fearfully and wonderfully made."

God is my advocate.

Whenever and however He wants to change me, it is for my good.

I will trust Him who forgives.

I will reject the lie that I am disqualified.

I will, likewise, reject the lie that my neighbor is disqualified as well.

---

135 Mark 16:7

DYING TO BE RIGHT

"A man dies when he refuses to stand up for that which is right."
—Dr. Martin Luther King Jr.

Would you like to live forever?

How many of you want the resurrection life Jesus promised?

Those of us who know Him certainly do! But you can't have resurrection life until you're dead!

Did Paul the apostle say, "I die monthly—when the bills come in?" "I die yearly—during tax season?"

No. He said, "I die daily!"

How often do you die?

As little as possible?

How can you tell if you're dead to your own will?

Consider these answers:

- ...when you're asleep in a boat in the middle of a storm.
- ...when someone slaps you on one cheek, and you turn the other one.
- ...when all hell breaks loose outside, and total peace reigns inside.

Resurrection Life!

It's what Sacramento needs.

It's what we all need.

Die to self and receive it!

I'm dying to myself and becoming alive to God, dying to the world and awakening to the Word. I've found that either I feed on the Word of God or the world feeds on me. So how do you get to know God? Give up the idea that you know what should happen. Allow Him to run the show by dying.

Paul the Apostle wrote, "I have been crucified with Christ. It is no longer I who live, but Christ who lives in me. And the life I now live in the flesh I live by faith in the Son of God, who loved me and gave himself for me."[136]

Walking is the art of balance.

It's learning to correct a continuous state of imbalance.

"Walking," like life, is a constant "mid-course correction."

It's a continuous acknowledgement of "I was wrong, but I want to make it right."

Isn't it funny, that after all the times we've blown it, we still have trouble admitting we're wrong?

Admitting we're wrong shouldn't be deflating.

It should be the most positive thing to do.

Walking is a continuous state of admitting, "I was heading in the wrong direction, but now I'm back on track." No one begins by mastering the "art of walking." Our first steps in life are always wobbly and unstable. But as time goes by, walking becomes steady.

Eventually... we can even carry others.

Sacramento needs an army of dead Christians who have received the resurrection power of Jesus and are willing to carry people of every nation, tribe, race, and language.

WHY CAPITALISM AND SOCIALISM AREN'T THE SOLUTION

"...power without love is reckless and abusive, and love without power is sentimental and anemic. Power at its best is love implementing the demands of justice, and justice at its best is power correcting everything that stands against love."

—Dr. Martin Luther King Jr.

I sincerely value all that public servants do to care for the complexity of needs within our society, but I have as much faith in politics and human governments being able to cure man's ills as Jesus did. Jesus knew the Kingdom of God was the answer to mankind's greatest needs, not the efforts of man.[137]

136 Galatians 2:20, ESV
137 Matthew 6:33

While there is no shortage of people talking about their version of freedom and truth, may we never forget what freedom and truth really are and from where they come.

Freedom and truth come from God alone.

Worldly seductions bring a temporary sense of freedom that always leads to bondage and depression. Man's attempts to redefine and then repackage truth only results in deception and lies.

Truth that transforms requires the compassionate courage to believe and do what God intended would set us free. Jesus said to the people who believed in Him, "You are truly My disciples if you remain faithful to My teachings. And you will know the truth, and the truth will set you free."[138]

Accept no earthly substitutes for truth and freedom.

They are only real if they are Heaven sent!

In a previous book I wrote this:

> "Either we return to the foundation of being under the ruler-ship of our Creator, or we eventually compromise every dimension of our lives.
>
> One of the saddest seductions of all is to look to man for the solution to life's dilemmas. From capitalists to communists, socialists to secularists, no political or economic system can keep self-indulgence and hypocrisy from raising their ugly heads. Excess and deceit are lodged in the human heart. Man playing God only makes it worse.
>
> When people grow weary of the greed of unscrupulous capitalists, they naively accept the thievery of socialists. The former system tends to seduce those who want more, which then makes little provision for those who have less. The latter structure penalizes the diligent, which then rewards the indolent. Either path is a ticking time bomb if the inner man is not transformed."[139]

138 John 8:31–32, NLT
139 Anfuso F. 2029: The Church of the Future. The Rock of Roseville; 2010.

Nor is government able to make us like or accept one another. Desegregation laws such as Affirmative Action have tried. The only solution is God's heart.

> *The Bible clearly asserts that it is the "heart that is deceitful above all things."*[140] *Only a commitment to follow the heart of God instills the compassion and community essential to create the society God intended and man longs for."*[141]

---

140 Jeremiah 17:9

141 Anfuso F. 2029: The Church of the Future. The Rock of Roseville; 2010.

FINISHING THE DREAM

"I have a dream that one day every valley shall be exalted, and every hill shall be made low; the crooked places shall be made straight, and the rough places plain; and the glory of the Lord shall be revealed, and all flesh shall see it together."

—Dr. Martin Luther King Jr.

I believe the primary reason Dr. King's dream was so widely received was because it was first birthed in the heart of God. If this statement is true, then we can have confidence the dream will be accomplished.

God always finishes what He starts.

Though there is significant value in you and I believing Dr. King's dream because it is God's dream, an infinitely more important question is: What is God's dream for you and me?

A nurse spent several years caring for patients during the last 12 weeks of their lives. She found the most common regret of those who were dying was: *"I wish I'd had the courage to live a life true to myself, not the life others expected of me."*

She reflected, *"When people realize that their life is almost over...it is easy to see how many dreams have gone unfulfilled. Most people had not honored even half of their dreams and had to die knowing that it was due to choices they had made, or not made."*[142]

One of the most wonderful effects of realizing God loves us just the way we are, is that it then gives us the liberty to be just that.

---

142 Ware B. The Top Five Regrets of the Dying. Hay House; 2012.

The Psalmist wrote, "I praise you, for I am fearfully and wonderfully made."[143] When we make the faith-choices God has asked us to, we can then see our dreams fulfilled.

There are many dangers in this world, but some are so treacherous they're called "evil." Evil! What could be so diabolical that God would call it evil, and yet so common that it infects all of us? The Book of Hebrews says, "Take care, brothers, lest there be in any of you an evil, unbelieving heart, leading you to fall away from the living God."[144]

WOW! That's scary!

Why would God call unbelief evil?

Because God is a God of faith—the opposite of unbelief.

He warns us to be careful because an unbelieving heart will lead us far away from the God who is life.

We have each been given a measure of eternal faith. It is most precious to God and should be guarded at all cost. It's the one thing to regularly mix with the Word of God. Without it, our lives cannot be transformed—never becoming who God created them to be.

The Bible says, "...the gospel was preached to us as well as to them; but the word which they heard did not profit them, not being mixed with faith in those who heard it."[145]

WOW! One thing was missing—faith!

And what does it take to activate faith? Courage! Dr. King finished living his dream with courage. Therefore, I'll let him define it for us:

> "Courage is an inner resolution to go forward despite
> obstacles; Cowardice is submissive surrender to circum-
> stances. Courage breeds creativity; Cowardice represses
> fear and is mastered by it. Cowardice asks the question, is
> it safe? Expediency asks the question, is it politic? Vanity
> asks the question, is it popular? But conscience asks the
> question, is it right? And there comes a time when we must
> take a position that is neither safe, nor politic, nor popular,
> but one must take it because it is right."[146]

---

143 Psalm 139:14, ESV
144 Hebrews 3:12, ESV
145 Hebrews 4:2 NKJV
146 Dr. Martin Luther King Jr.

THE LATINOS ARE COMING!

"God is not interested merely in freeing black men and brown men and yellow men, but God is interested in freeing the whole human race. We must work with determination to create a society, not where black men are superior and other men are inferior and vice versa, but a society in which all men will live together as brothers and respect the dignity and worth of human personality."

—*Dr. Martin Luther King Jr.*

In March of 2014, Latinos became the largest ethnic group in California (39 percent), surpassing whites (38.8 percent). This is the first time since California became a state in 1850 that Latinos compose the single largest racial or ethnic group. The only other state to cross this threshold is New Mexico.

It is likewise estimated that the Latino population will increase until they become America's most dominant ethnicity in 2043.[147]

God is not surprised by the changes happening around us and neither should we be.

What preparation can the church in America do?

What bridges can we build?

What breaches can we heal?

What racial divide can we span in Sacramento to unify the races in the one and only kingdom of God?

A truly prophetic people are to be the head and not the tail.[148]

May we embrace the future with open arms of hope and absolute conviction that it will be better, not worse.

The Church should be the first ones to position for change.

What a golden opportunity in Sacramento is before us!

How would Jesus connect the fragmented parts of His Body in our region?

---

147 Kayne E. Census: White majority in U.S. gone by 2043. NBC News. Retrieved from: http://usnews. nbcnews.com/_news/2013/06/13/18934111-census-white-majority-in-us-gone-by-2043 on August 15, 2014.
148 Deuteronomy 28:13

How would Jesus love the least, laying down His life in whatever way necessary to rescue those in need or to communicate His love today?

If we ask, He will give us the answers to these most pressing questions. The Bible promises, "If any of you lacks wisdom, let him ask of God...and it will be given to him."[149]

California is God's crucible, a melting pot of races, the flavors of Heaven's sons and daughters blended together.

WE WERE BORN FOR TROUBLE!

"Worship at its best is a social experience with people of all levels of life coming together to realize their oneness and unity under God. Whenever the church, consciously or unconsciously caters to one class it loses the spiritual force of the 'whosoever will, let him come' doctrine and is in danger of becoming a little more than a social club with a thin veneer of religiosity."

—Dr. Martin Luther King Jr.

We were born for trouble! And it's very likely that trouble is up ahead as we seek to unify our region.

But, trouble molds our souls into the image of God!

I admit I don't know what's best. If I did, I'd bail a friend out of every crisis he ever encountered. If it were up to me, I'd spoil the whole planet. But there are some problems that shouldn't be fixed because God doesn't want them fixed.

Sometimes He's even the author of our problems.

God is far more interested in fixing us than fixing problems.

We attempt projects while God says, "You're the project! I'm working on you!"

We're saying, "God, stop the problem!" He's saying, "Begin to understand what I'm doing." At one point, Jesus said, "Now my soul is deeply troubled. Should I pray, 'Father, save me from this hour'? But this is the very reason I came!"[150]

---

149 James 1:5, NKJV
150 John 12:27, NLT

The Bible even adds, *"And being in agony He prayed more earnestly."*[151]

Thank God for your troubles because they are shaping you into the person you were created to be. Thank God for the struggles that are part of bringing Heaven to Earth.

You were made for this war! I'm talking about spiritual war.

The Bible assures us that God's Spirit will give us the strength we need to tear down strongholds in Sacramento, uproot lies across communities, and have hearts and minds filled with eternal truth in our churches. God promises to set us free.

So don't resist or fear the struggle. Embrace it! If you respond well it will bring out your best and pave the way toward the vision.

Our loving Creator who, before we breathed even one breath or fought a single battle, determined *"...in all these things we are (called to be) more than conquerors through Him who loved us."*[152]

What exactly does spiritual war look like?

Perhaps those who have lived the longest would know best.

A study was done that determined the four convictions to which people who live to 100 years old adhere. I believe each one has a spiritual counterpart.

First: being optimistic and having a positive attitude. Paul the Apostle wrote, *"...He who has begun a good work in you will complete it"*[153]

Secondly: continuing to be engaged with purpose, vision, and activity. *"For where there is no vision, the people perish."*[154]

Thirdly: staying flexible and involved in physical activity. In God's creation we can see that trees, which are healthy, have flexible branches.

151 Luke 22:44, NKJV
152 Romans 8:37, NKJV
153 Philippians 1:6, NKJV
154 Proverbs 29:18, NKJV

And lastly: learning to deal with loss. Paul again wrote, "...For His sake I have suffered the loss of all things and count them as rubbish, in order that I may gain Christ."[155]

Isn't it fascinating that people who practice these biblical practices live longer?

WHOEVER HAS THE MOST HOPE...WINS!

"I'm not going to put my ultimate faith in the little gods that can be destroyed in an atomic age, but the God who has been our help in ages past, and our hope for years to come, and our shelter in the time of storm, and our eternal home. That's the God that I'm putting my ultimate faith in."

—Dr. Martin Luther King Jr.

We face battle every day.

Struggles vacillate between hope and concern.

Is your heart filled with more hope or more concern?

Would you visit a doctor who expressed more concern about your health without offering equal hope?

How about God?

When He thinks of you, is He more concerned or more hopeful?

It's an important question, one that ought to be weighed before you join His battle force because it will shape your attitudes and joy.

The Bible doesn't say God is a God of concern, it says emphatically He's a God of hope. *"Now may the God of hope fill you with all joy and peace in believing, that you may abound in hope by the power of the Holy Spirit."*[156]

Are you disillusioned about your life, your community, and your culture? Frustrated because something's not happening?

---

155 Philippians 3:8, ESV
156 Romans 15:13, NKJV

Disillusionment occurs when reality doesn't match hopes and expectations. At times it's because we think our best days are behind us; we believe our past mistakes have disqualified us from a great future; we think we'll never be happy.

Something's terribly wrong when we don't look forward to getting up in the morning; when we don't love the life God's given us; when we believe lies.

The truth is no past mistake can disqualify us from the wonderful plan God has for our work in His kingdom. God has our future in His all-caring, all-powerful hands and He is rooting for us to succeed. As the Psalmist wrote, "This I know, that God is for me."[157]

At times I've wondered if God is moving in some people's lives more than others. God wants to move in each of our lives equally, but He can work only in me if I allow Him. So yes, God moves in some people's lives more than others. Why? Because God responds to faith! The Bible says in the book of Hebrews, "...without faith it is impossible to please God..."[158] and then in the book of James, "Draw near to God and He will draw near to you."[159]

Faith draws us closer to what we believe, while fear pushes us further away.

God builds His kingdom on faith.

Satan establishes his on fear.

Both faith and fear are unknowns.

Our actions reflect one or the other.

Fear prompts us to cower and worry about the future.

Faith calls us forward to trust God for every resource.

It's our choice.

Don't react to a fear-based economy. Rather, respond in faith to His Word that says, "...my God will meet all your needs according to His glorious riches in Christ Jesus."

157 Psalm 56:9, NKJV
158 Hebrews 11:6, NKJV
159 James 4:8, NKJV

We wonder why certain things happen...some good and some bad. Is anyone behind the wheel of our lives...anyone guiding and watching over our souls?

The truth is, there are no accidental sparrows or snowflakes, no coincidental moments or mountains to climb. The glorious God continuously contemplates every molecule in the Universe, but none more special than the ones that make up His sons and daughters.

Everything God intends for Sacramento must be immersed in faith, hope and love.

But here's the key when it comes to these eternal three: God is love! Everything He does is based upon His true nature: LOVE! Therefore everything we hope for Sacramento can only bear lasting fruit if it is birthed in God's love.

You and I have been called to act in faith, hope and love for such a time as this!

CHAPTER 12

A CITY THAT LOOKS LIKE HEAVEN

*"...life at its best is a creative synthesis of
opposites in fruitful harmony."*

—Dr. Martin Luther King Jr.

What would it take for a city to look like Heaven?

That's an easy question. A miracle!

Is it an accident that we who live in Sacramento are surrounded by exceptional racial diversity, or is it the ball being teed up for a miracle to come to Earth?

That's exactly what happened just before the birth of the church. The apostles were hopelessly divided, and when Jesus needed them the most, they all headed for the hills.

But then it happened.

The greatest miracle of all time, the resurrection of Jesus from the dead, struck like a lightning bolt from Heaven. A paradigm shift to end all—reset the clock. It was a new day...really, a new age! Suddenly, lesser impossibilities were now lined up to land. All that was needed was faith to believe; to believe that all of the lousy attitudes and responses the apostles had given into were now covered by the blood of Jesus. In a tiny upper room Heaven would touch Earth! In my imagination, I can see tears of forgiveness; the posturing that was so prevalent before the Crucifixion was now covered by the humility that was so rare.

"...suddenly there came from heaven a sound like a mighty rushing wind, and it filled the entire house where they were sitting."[160] A supernatural, breach-healing language transcended geographies and ethnicities. The Bible recounts the astonishment of the multi-racial masses. "Parthians and Medes and Elamites and residents of Mesopotamia, Judea and Cappadocia, Pontus and Asia, Phrygia and Pamphylia, Egypt and the parts of Libya belonging to Cyrene, and visitors from Rome, both Jews and proselytes, Cretans and Arabians—we hear them telling in our own tongues the mighty works of God."[161]

When the disciples gave up the petty, the grand was waiting to envelop them. When they allowed the unity of divine love to overflow their hearts, suddenly the Kingdom of Heaven could no longer restrain itself.

Heaven came to Earth to join the party.

Even now, Heaven longs to finish the miracle of reconciliation, and we are the tipping point to make it happen. Will we allow God's love to flow from the river of life into our hearts? One person at a time? One conversation, one hug, one word of forgiveness at a time?

The suddenlies of God will once again burst forth to rescue.

When Moses and three million Israelites journeyed through the wilderness, miracles were a constant. Every day they needed 1,500 tons of food, 4,000 tons of wood for cooking, and 11,000,000 gallons of water for drinking and washing.

They needed all of this each and every day for 40 years.

No one knows our needs more than God. And no one wants to help more than He does. So we must not be afraid to ask Him for what He does best: miracles. Jesus said, *"Ask and it will be given to you; seek and you will find; knock and the door will be opened to you."*[162]

WHEN THE DISCIPLES GAVE UP THE PETTY, THE GRAND WAS WAITING TO ENVELOP THEM.

When we look back from eternity we will realize the greatest moments in our lives were miracles...Heaven touching Earth.

For many people the greatest miracle that could ever happen to them would be winning the lottery.

---

160 Acts 2:2, ESV
161 Acts 2:9–11, NKJV
162 Matthew 7:7, NIV

Watching my father die when I was 17 years old having achieved riches and fame, and yet still noticeably unfulfilled, freed me from any pursuit of either.

I want to be rich and famous in eternity!

If relational riches are what God calls true wealth, then we can and should seek them with all our heart. Pursuing riches is a great ambition...as long as the wealth lasts forever. Though we can't take earthly riches with us, we can send them on ahead. John Wesley said, "We should only value things by the price they shall gain in eternity."

Eternity is the main event!

Earth is a mere dress rehearsal!

The Bible says, "Think about the things of heaven, not the things of earth. For you died to this life, and your real life is hidden with Christ in God."[163]

ETERNITY IS THE MAIN EVENT! EARTH IS A MERE DRESS REHEARSAL!

Jesus reminded us of this when He said, "The Kingdom of Heaven is like a treasure that a man discovered hidden in a field. In his excitement, he hid it again and sold everything he owned to get enough money to buy the field."[164]

The greatest joys in life are eternal, and God has prepared them for each of us right where we live.

I want to see the riches of Heaven in Sacramento's people. I want to remember the treasures of God's mercy and selfless love extended to me. They are the pearls that will inspire me to honor with humility those from other races and cultures.

One night, when I was struggling with pressures, the Lord replayed memories of the many times He'd saved me from near-death experiences: the out of control "360" on an icy highway; the galloping horse that barely skidded to a stop on a muddy field; when, on an hallucinogenic, a friend grabbed my arm to keep me from jumping hundreds of feet off a Rocky Mountain cliff into Class 5 Rapids I thought looked like marshmallows; the desperate time as a suicidal atheist I wandered into a desert to cut my wrist and end my life.

---

163 Colossians 3:2–3, NLT
164 Matthew 13:44, NLT

Over and over again He reminded me of His saving grace... His unfailing love... *"His merciful kindness, which is so great toward us."*[165]

"Through the LORD'S mercies we are not consumed, because His compassions fail not."[166]

I'm blessed...with a bright future! So are you!

Sacramento is blessed with a bright future, if we can once again discover the relational gold that lies just beneath the surface.

And there's enough Heavenly gold to make us each rich.

SACRAMENTO: AMERICA'S MELTING POT

"The church, itself, will stand under the judgment of God. Now that the mistake of the past has been made, I think that the opportunity of the future is to really go out and to transform American society, and where else is there a better place than in the institution that should serve as the moral guardian of the community. The institution that should preach brotherhood and make it a reality within its own body."[167]

—Dr. Martin Luther King Jr.

There are a number of confirming indicators that God has sovereignly been at work in the Sacramento region. Consider the ramifications of the following divinely orchestrated historic and contemporary events related to Sacramento.

1. California was founded prior to the Civil War as a free state. Its very origin is a statement of divine intent.

2. Sacramento founding pastors led the charge for racial equality for early Chinese and African-American residents. Our resolute heritage calls to us. May we hear this generational cry, fully embrace our heritage, and step into our destiny.

3. California's first civilian Governor and United States Senator, John Fremont, was a devout Christian. He advocated for racial justice and refused personal gain, the real possibility of becoming President of the United States. Instead, he and his wife stood for what was right, not what would benefit them.

---

165 Psalm 117:2

166 Lamentations 3:22, NKJV

167 "Social Justice and the Emerging New Age" address at the Herman W. Read Fieldhouse, Western Michigan University. December 18, 1963.

4. The fact that Sacramento is presently *"America's Most Racially Diverse City"*[168] is both a privilege and opportunity for unprecedented breakthrough. Yet, without the Body of Christ's whole-hearted commitment, there are no guarantees for success. The church of Jesus Christ must willingly build bridges of selfless love and genuine friendship. We must even consider what might be a strategic disadvantage in the hope of demonstrating God's heart. Remember Jesus' sacrifice on the cross. A region, created to be a melting pot of heavenly diversity, awaits our decision.

5. Two global moves of God have previously originated in California. [1]Six hundred million Pentecostal Christians claim their spiritual heritage from the Azusa Street Revival of 1906. Spearheaded by an African-American, this mighty work began with a significant multi-racial emphasis. [2]The *Jesus Movement* of the late 1960's also began in Southern California. It ushered as many as three million primarily young people, from seventy countries, into the Kingdom of God.

6. The present breakthroughs in the Sacramento region related to unity and racial harmony amongst church leaders and believers clearly indicate that there is grace for further advancement of the Kingdom of God.

7. Two regional events celebrating Dr. King's life and message take place annually in Sacramento. The *MLK Celebration at Capital Christian Center* and the *MLK: March For The Dream* in downtown Sacramento are attended by thousands, and serve as powerful catalysts for racial harmony.

Near the end of Christ's earthly ministry He wept over Jerusalem because its inhabitants didn't know the way of peace God had chosen for them. He was broken-hearted that they would soon be destroyed and their children with them. This was primarily because they didn't know their time of visitation—their hour of divine opportunity.[169]

---

168 Stodghill R, Bower A. Welcome to America's Most Diverse City. TIME. August 25, 2002. Retrieved from: http://content.time.com/time/nation/article/0,8599,340694,00.html#ixzz2rcHHuep9 on August 9, 2014.
169 Luke 19:41–44

What additional wells of awakening does God intend for California, the most strategic state in the world's most influential nation?

What role will Sacramento have in leading the way?

VALUES AND DESTINY

"You are not only responsible for what you say, but also for what you do not say."

—Dr. Martin Luther King Jr.

Our values control our destiny. Our values in Sacramento will dictate not only what we believe, but also how you live! Before determining tenets to guide our lives, we must see them in the light of eternity. From where do we adopt values? From only two places: the world or the Word.

IF WE FOLLOW THE WORLD AND NOT THE WORD, WE'LL MISS THE MINE AND GET THE SHAFT.

If we follow the world and not the Word, we'll miss the mine and get the shaft.

The world or culture often focuses on what we can get. Jesus came to serve and not be served. He came to give and not to receive. This is why the Bible says so clearly, don't imitate the culture's morality, don't *"...be conformed to this world, but be transformed by the renewing of your mind, that you may prove what is good and acceptable and the perfect will of God."*[170]

Heaven and Earth will eventually pass away, but God's Word will last forever.[171] The apostle Paul knew exactly why he was alive, He said, *"For to me, to live is Christ..."*[172]

What drives your life? What moves you? What are you living for? What would you say? *"For me to live is shopping, or NFL football?" "For me to live is my children or my career?"* We see what we live for, our treasure, in what we give our heart to. Jesus said, *"...seek first the kingdom of God and His righteousness, and all these things shall be added to you."*[173]

---

170 Romans 12:2, NKJV
171 Matthew 24:35
172 Philippians 1:21, NKJV
173 Matthew 6:33, NKJV

God promises to meet our needs if our focus is on Jesus and advancing His Kingdom right here in Sacramento. Know this for sure: only our Creator can perfectly guide and bless our lives.

MAKING YOUR LIFE A "GET TO"

"And when you discover what you will be in your life, set out to do it as if God Almighty called you at this particular moment in history to do it. Don't just set out to do a good job. Set out to do such a good job that the living, the dead or the unborn couldn't do it any better. If it falls to your lot to be a street sweeper, sweep streets like Michelangelo painted pictures, sweep streets like Beethoven composed music … Sweep streets like Shakespeare wrote poetry. Sweep streets so well that all the host of heaven and earth will have to pause and say: Here lived a great street sweeper who swept his job well."

—*Dr. Martin Luther King Jr.*

What kind of being is God? He's a giver!

Not a grandstanding giver, but one who gives in obscurity. As God is a giver, so He created us to be givers as well, but to give in the way He models every day—invisibly! It's easy to take that for granted. Spotlights don't advertise God's generosity. *"This morning's sunrise is brought to you by God,"* or flowers stamped, *"Made in Heaven."*

Jesus said, *"Give, and it will be given to you..."*[174]

God could have said, *"Give, and don't ask Me why! Give, or else!"* God motivates us to change with love and rewards. That's why He said, *"Give, and it will be given to you..."*

It's the goodness of God that inspires us to change.[175]

Today resist seeing obedience to God as a "have to." Instead see obedience as a "get to," a glorious gift.

Does God have to give? Absolutely not! He owns everything!

---

174 Luke 6:38, NKJV
175 Romans 2:4

God gives because He loves people. A divinely created people have captured His heart, and now He invites us to join Him in learning to love them as He loves them.

Not selected people, not people only like us, we are called to love all people, no matter who they are or what they have done...unconditionally!

The Bible says, *"The earth is the Lord's, and everything in it. The world and all its people belong to Him."*[176]

What a privilege we have before us! We have one of the greatest cross-sections of people found anywhere on Earth.

Yet every blessing God bestows is because of His grace. "Every good gift and every perfect gift is from above, and comes down from the Father of lights..."

God is looking for people who are willing to distribute his products: His love, His joy, His peace, His forgiveness, and His kindness.

In Heaven will there be any boasting about the good we have done? Why would there be? If our motives or actions genuinely contained anything inherently good, then God gave it, since Jesus said, "No one is good—except God alone."

So rejoice in your hidden prayers, your invisible acts of kindness, building bridges wherever races are divided, and offering healing words where harsh words have hurt.

---

176 Psalm 24:1, NLT

HISTORY, DESTINY, LEGACY

"Like anybody, I would like to have a long life. Longevity has its place. But I'm not concerned about that now. I just want to do God's will."

—Dr. Martin Luther King Jr.

If you want to envision the path before you, study the one you have followed.

Your foundation holds the key to your future. Our History of advocacy and justice in Sacramento will lead to our Destiny and ultimate Legacy.

In the Book of Genesis, the book of beginnings, Abraham's son Isaac realized the key to his future was inexorably tied to his father's past. He re-dug what his father had started. When Isaac did this, God opened up a spring of fresh water in a new well.

> *"...Isaac dug again the wells of water that had been dug in the days of Abraham his father, which the Philistines had stopped after the death of Abraham. And he gave them the names that his father had given them. But when Isaac's servants dug in the valley and found there a well of spring water..."* [177]

Perhaps a new well of fresh water will bring a mighty move of God that we have been praying for throughout our region and nation.

Perhaps bringing the Body of Christ together as His family will put a smile on the face of God and bring an outpouring of His Spirit.

Perhaps recognizing we cannot fulfill our personal destiny until we join to fulfill those of the Body of Christ.

Perhaps as we esteem others as more important than ourselves, we will represent Jesus so well, the world will know that we truly belong to Him.

---

[177] Genesis 26:18–19, ESV

Perhaps Sacramento is America's most racially diverse city because God wants us to end racism in America—to link our providential past with our prophetic future!

Jesus promised, "Whoever believes in me, as Scripture has said, rivers of living water will flow from within them."[178]

May it flow within each of us, every day!

We should have no greater prayer than this.

---

178 John 7:38

ADDENDUM

I close this book with a final quote from Dr. Martin Luther King Jr. As a representative of all minorities in our modern day, He so eloquently and emotionally outlined the plight of our African-American brothers and sisters from generations past, linking their history and pain with their future victory and hope.

> *"Abused and scorned though we may be, our destiny is tied up with America's destiny. Before the pilgrims landed at Plymouth, we were here. Before the pen of Jefferson etched the majestic words of the Declaration of Independence across the pages of history, we were here. For more than two centuries our forebears labored in this country without wages; they made cotton king; they built the homes of their masters while suffering gross injustice and shameful humiliation—and yet out of a bottomless vitality they continued to thrive and develop. If the inexpressible cruelties of slavery could not stop us, the opposition we now face will surely fail. We will win our freedom because the sacred heritage of our nation and the eternal will of God are embodied in our echoing demands."*[179]

Though Dr. King's life was cut short, the "March For The Dream" continues because it was never his dream.

It is God's!

---

[179] Letter from a Birmingham Jail, 1963

"A CITY THAT LOOKS LIKE HEAVEN" SMALL GROUPS WITH VIDEOS

This book and accompanying videos may be used in an Eight-Week, Small Group format. Here are the recommended small group structure and weekly assignments.

TIMEFRAME

90 minutes, either weekly or bi-monthly

LOCATION

Though a singular location is often most convenient, moving the small group from home to home will also provide shared experience.

FELLOWSHIP, WORSHIP, AND PRAYER

Group Discussion may be preceded or followed by fellowship, worship and prayer.

INTER-RACIAL SMALL GROUPS

We recommend that small groups be inter-racial as much as possible. This will provide a broader cross-section of dialogue during discussion times. The racial breakthroughs we hope for can only occur as every wall of division is torn down and bridges of loving relationships are established.

REVIEW VIDEOS

Each small group participant, prior to reading the weekly assigned section, can view the designated video(s) online at www.citylikeheaven.com. Another option would be to view the assigned video during your small group. Likewise, participants may view each video on their mobile devices with the QR Reader App (Barcode Scanner).

WEEK ONE

Chapter 1 Why the Book Title?
Chapter 2 The Clearest Voice In the 20th Century Still Speaks in the 21st Century

VIDEO #1: "MLK—March for the Dream" video

SCRIPTURES
Hebrews 11:10, Matthew 6:9, Genesis 1:27, Revelation 7:9, Matthew 22:37–38

QUOTE FROM CHAPTERS 1 & 2
Was Dr. King naïve when he wrote this from a Birmingham jail?

"Perhaps I have once again been too optimistic. Is organized religion too inextricably bound to the status quo to save our nation and the world? Perhaps I must turn my faith to the inner spiritual church, the church within the church, as the true ekklesia and the hope of the world. But again I am thankful to God that some noble souls from the ranks of organized religion have broken loose from the paralyzing chains of conformity and joined us as active partners in the struggle for freedom."

CHAPTERS 1 & 2 — QUESTIONS FOR DISCUSSION

1. What is your response to the life and message of Dr. Martin Luther King Jr.?

2. Do you believe God the Father has no greater desire than for His children to love one another?

3. Has God been stirring your faith to believe for healing of racial divisions?

4. What do you think of the fact that the majority of millennials see themselves as post-racial?

5. Can you imagine racism in America ending in your lifetime?

WEEK TWO

Chapter 3 Visiting Mt. Rushmore But Never Seeing It
Chapter 4 California and Slavery

VIDEO #2: "Spiritual History of Sacramento"

SCRIPTURES
2 Kings 17:26–28, John 3:17, Galatians 6:10, Luke 10:25–37

QUOTES FROM CHAPTERS 3 & 4
Consider the ramifications of the following quotes:

> *"Until I care for what God cares for, I can't live the life He intended me to live!"*

> *"...none of us have been short-changed. All of us have been lavishly overpaid."*

Would the Bible concur with Dr. King's quote: "Our loyalties must transcend our race, our tribe, our class, and our nation; and this means we must develop a world perspective."

CHAPTERS 3 & 4 — QUESTIONS FOR DISCUSSION

1. Do you see ways in which your own selfishness has fueled racial division?

2. How does the fact that Sacramento's founding pastors and prominent political leaders having advocated for racial equality encourage you to live today?

3. Can you name additional situations in the Bible in which God exposed racial injustices?

4. How do you respond to racial injustice happening around you?

5. Do you see yourself as soft-minded or strong-minded? Why?

 # WEEK THREE

Chapter 5 Living In America's Most Racially Diverse City
Chapter 6 When Are You Going To Come To Us?

VIDEO #3: "End Racism In America"

SCRIPTURES
Ephesians 4:32, Luke 7:47, Matthew 5:14, Isaiah 58:12, Luke 4:18, 2 Corinthians 5:18, Ephesians 2:10, James 2:14–18

QUOTES FROM CHAPTERS 5 & 6
Were you personally challenged by this question from Bishop Sherwood Carthen, *"We are always coming to you. When are you going to come to us?"*

Is this quote by Dr. Martin Luther King Jr. taken from the "Letter From the Birmingham Jail" still relevant today? *"Injustice anywhere is a threat to justice everywhere. We are caught in an inescapable network of mutuality, tied in a single garment of destiny. Whatever affects one directly, affects all indirectly."*

CHAPTERS 5 & 6 — QUESTIONS FOR DISCUSSION

1. Does the fact that Sacramento is the most racially diverse region in America give it a special responsibility to build bridges between races?

2. Can you share an experience of public support or endorsement of a race other than your own where you were the only one of your race present?

3. Have you ever heard someone say of another ethnicity, "They need to get over it!"?

4. For a person of a majority race: How has God convicted you about giving up on people from another race?

5. For a person of a minority race: How has God convicted you about giving up on people from another race?

WEEK FOUR

Chapter 7 Believing for the Impossible

VIDEO #4: "Unstoppable!"

SCRIPTURES
Matthew 19:26, Hebrews 11:1, 3, 8, Matthew 19:26,
2 Corinthians 12:9

QUOTE FROM CHAPTER 7
Is there any dimension in your life where you are *"...absolutely certain that nothing less than the impossible would meet the need"?* What impossibility is God asking you to believe for?

Do you really believe this Hudson Taylor quote is true?
"First it is impossible. Then it is difficult. Then it is done."
Or is it overstated?

CHAPTER 7 — QUESTIONS FOR DISCUSSION

1. What impossible situation in the Bible has most impacted you?

2. Have you seen God do something impossible to heal a relational breach in your own life?

3. What impossible situation is God presently asking you to believe for?

4. Do you sense a fresh anointing on unity between churches and leaders in this region?

5. Are you presently stepping up, choosing to obey the Lord, and doing something that is very difficult? If yes, what is it?

WEEK FIVE

Chapter 8 The One Thing You Could Do

VIDEO #5: "The Skin We Live In"

SCRIPTURES
Ezekiel 36:26, Leviticus 19:34, Hebrews 13:2, 1 Peter 2:17, Matthew 6:3, Philippians 2:3–4, Romans 12:10, 1 John 4:20–21, John 3:30

QUOTE FROM CHAPTER 8
What do you think about the principle demonstrated in the following story? "(When) A bi-lingual pastor... meets a Mexican-American he asks them, 'Has anyone welcomed you to America since you've been here?' Invariably they will say, 'No!' Then with a big smile, and total sincerity, he says, 'I'm so sorry that hasn't happened yet. Let me be then the first to say to you, 'Welcome to America! We're glad you're here!' The response to this heart-felt word is often shocking. Smiles come to faces, tears to eyes."

CHAPTER 8 — QUESTIONS FOR DISCUSSION

1. What one act could you do to help end racism in America?

2. How has God rescued you? Are you grateful?

3. Can you name a little thing that someone did for you that changed your world in BIG way?

4. Could you imagine yourself verbally welcoming an immigrant to America?

5. Does the idea that God asks us to be invisible at times make sense to you?

WEEK SIX

Chapter 9 One Friend at a Time
Chapter 10 Being Right is Overrated

VIDEO #6: "Journey 2 Mosaic"

SCRIPTURES
Matthew 5:43–45, Jeremiah 31:3, Psalm 139:14,
1 Corinthians 9:19, 22–23, John 8:31–32, Jeremiah 17:9,
Matthew 22:37–40

QUOTE FROM CHAPTERS 9 &10
What do you think about this quote from Dr. King? "Love is understanding, redemptive goodwill for all men, so that you love everybody, because God loves them. You refuse to do anything that will defeat an individual, because you have agape in your soul. And here you come to the point that you love the individual who does the evil deed, while hating the deed that the person does. This is what Jesus means when he says, 'Love your enemy.' This is the way to do it. When the opportunity presents itself when you can defeat your enemy, you must not do it."

CHAPTERS 9 & 10 — QUESTIONS FOR DISCUSSION

1. Are you presently building a relational bridge with someone from another race?

2. Do you battle with thoughts of insignificance to God? What is the truth?

3. Can you think of a situation where God asked you to love someone you thought was an enemy?

4. What phraseology do you use when you refer to other races. Why?

5. Do you believe that capitalism or socialism is the solution?

WEEK SEVEN

Chapter 11 Finishing the Dream

VIDEO #7: "Racial Reconciliation Panel"

SCRIPTURES
Psalm 139:14, Luke 4:19, John 12:27, Romans 8:37, Philippians 1:6, Proverbs 29:18, Philippians 3:8, Romans 15:13, Psalm 56:9, Hebrews 11:6, Philippians 4:19, Psalm 43:5

QUOTE FROM CHAPTER 11
What do you think of this statistic and projection?

"In March of 2014, Latinos became the largest ethnic group in California (39%), surpassing whites (38.8%). This is the first time since California became a state in 1850 that Latinos are the single largest racial or ethnic group. The only other state to cross this threshold is New Mexico. It is likewise estimated that the Latino population will increase until they become America's most dominant ethnicity in 2043. "

CHAPTER 11 — QUESTIONS FOR DISCUSSION

1. What would finishing Dr. Martin Luther King's dream look like?

2. How do you feel about Latinos becoming the most dominant race in California and eventually America?

3. Do you believe God specifically prepares great struggles in order to form you into the person He desires you to be? Name one.

4. Are you more concerned or hopeful about your future?

5. Are you primarily concerned about the next generation, or are you more hopeful?

 **WEEK EIGHT**

Chapter 12 A City That Looks Like Heaven

VIDEO #8: "A City That Looks Like Heaven"

SCRIPTURES
Colossians 3:2-3, Matthew 13:44, Matthew 6:33, Romans 2:4, Luke 6:38, Romans 2:4, Psalm 24:1, James 1:17, Genesis 26:18-19, John 7:38

QUOTE FROM CHAPTER 12
How does this quote impact you, "Near the end of Christ's earthly ministry He wept over Jerusalem because its inhabitants didn't know the way of peace God had chosen for them. He was broken-hearted that they would soon be destroyed, and their children with them. This was primarily because they didn't know their time of visitation— their hour of divine opportunity."

CHAPTER 12 — QUESTIONS FOR DISCUSSION

1. Do you really believe God desires your city to look like Heaven?

2. How have your values shaped your destiny in a positive or negative way?

3. Do you see the things God has called you to do as "have to's" or "get to's"?

4. In what way might Sacramento's history of racial justice connect to your present destiny?

5. How do you feel about offering love and appreciation to other races as part of God's intention for Sacramento's legacy?

RECOMMENDED BOOKS
OTHER TITLES BY FRANCIS ANFUSO

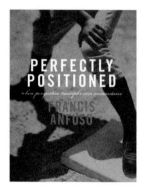

Perfectly Positioned—
When Perspective Triumphs Over Circumstance*
Do you wish God had written a different script for you? Do you see your life as an exquisite feast or burnt toast? Are you eating and enjoying every bite or is it boring, bland and predictable? Are you filled with regret and shame or hope and healing? Our lives begin to be truly transformed when we stop asking God to change our circumstances, and allow Him to change our perspective! Behind every challenging situation there is a loving God whose victorious perspective is far greater than the trials we face. God's will is that we would embrace the life He has given us, instead of wishing for what does not exist and would not satisfy even if it did. If you have come to the realization that you have fished all night and caught nothing, it is not an accident. Keep fishing! God has perfectly positioned you to read this book. The breakthrough you have been longing for is just ahead!

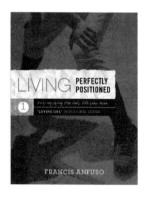

Living Perfectly Positioned—
"Loving Life" Devotional Series
This book could be called: "The Greatest Hits of Perfectly Positioned." The best of the best revelations are in bite-size, one-a-day pieces. Instead of wishing you had a different script for your life, God can renew your mind to enjoy the only life you have. By changing your perspective, you will see your life changed! God's will is that we would embrace the life He has given us, instead of wishing for what does not exist and would not satisfy even if it did. If you have come to the realization that you have fished all night and caught nothing, it's not an accident. Keep fishing! God has perfectly positioned you to read this book. The breakthrough you have been longing for is just ahead!

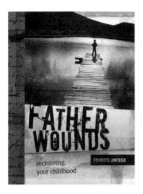

Father Wounds—Reclaiming Your Childhood*

As an abandoned and abused son, my soul suffered long-term destruction. But my wounded heart was exactly what God wanted to heal and restore. I discovered God is the Father I always wanted. He's the perfect Dad I needed all along. God can help you forgive the parent who hurt you. He wants to heal you completely and use you mightily in the lives of others! Today is the day to step into the wholeness and destiny God has for His children!

2029—The Church of the Future*

You can comprehend the future if you study the past and discern the present. God is not hiding what is about to happen. He longs to reveal it to us. In 1989, Francis Anfuso wrote We've Got a Future—The 21st Century Church. Now, two decades after its release, the book reads like a detailed depiction of today's church. But the story is far from finished. This next volume details what is about to unfold—where the church must go, and the significant role you can play. 2029 is a glimpse into our future. A taste of what will shortly come to pass. Now is not the time for the Church to shrink back and recoil as the battle rages. Instead, we are approaching our finest hour.

Church Wounds—
Francis Anfuso and David Loveless*

Our wounds don't have to disable us. They're meant to be a doorway into the restored life God always intended. God wants to heal us, if we want to be. For God to free us, we must allow Him to touch our pain. Church Wounds examines the most common hurts inflicted by Christians on Christians: hypocrisy, judgmentalism, leader insensitivities, and abuse, plus many more. Read the stories of those who were not just hurt—but healed; and then experience the healing yourself.

NUMB

We all fight numbness and its long-term effect. Unless our daily reality is greater than our inner fantasy, we'll wander from one reality-replacement to another. When we forget what we know—we forfeit who we are.

Everything God does is designed to lead us into intimacy with Him—to set us free from boredom, loneliness, and self-absorbed distractions. He loves us enough to allow us to be satisfied with only Himself.

Identity / Destiny Prayer Journal

The first step in fulfilling your destiny is finding your identity, and only God knows the answer to this question. My true identity is who He created me to be. My ultimate destiny is what He has called me to do. In our natural life we will only see what we are willing to focus upon. But…"In prayer there is a connection between what God does and what you do." Matthew 6:14 (MSG) It is in prayer that God helps us understand Him in fresh ways and deeper levels. We connect with Him and He unlocks His kingdom within us. Inside this 40-Day Prayer Journal you will examine areas of life that will call for new focus and connected prayer. In so doing, you will experience the endlessly delightful relationship He promises.

revivalstories.org

Why do we need a revival? Because a revival does what only God can do. Revival is when God springs a convicting surprise on His creation — it's when Jesus is so lifted up, He draws multitudes to Himself. At revivalstories.org, you can access powerful videos describing some of the greatest revival moments throughout history. From the Great Awakenings to the great evangelists and revivalists, revival stories unlocks the heartbeat of the why and how of revivals. When a generation gets so desperate for Jesus to transform their culture that Christians finally humble themselves, and cry out in desperation for God to intervene.

AWAKENED

What would it take to:

- awaken a nation that has ceased to depend upon God?
- awaken the mind of those who no longer fear or reverence Him?
- awaken the conscience of those who have grown numb to discerning good and evil?
- awaken the hearts of those who consider it a choice to end the lives of their unborn children, while rejecting God's order for marriage and the family?
- revive the spirit of a church that has grown sleepy and indifferent toward the broken world around them?

What would it take? It would take a move of God... a revival of Biblical proportions! Rekindle your passion for Jesus and prepare for the sovereign outpouring we so desperately need. May we each find our unique role for all that is ahead and be fully protected during the ensuing battle.